The First Year as Principal

The First Year as Principal

Real World Stories from America's Principals

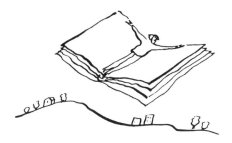

Edited by
Ronald Thorpe

HEINEMANN
PORTSMOUTH, NH

Heinemann
A division of Reed Elsevier Inc.
361 Hanover St.
Portsmouth, NH 03801-3912
Offices and agents throughout the world

Library of Congress Cataloging-in-Publication Data
The first year as principal : real world stories from America's
    principals / edited by Ronald Thorpe.
        p.   cm.
    ISBN 0-435-08128-4 (alk. paper). — ISBN 0-435-08127-6 (pbk.)
    1. School principals—United States.   2. School management and
organization—United States.   I. Thorpe, Ronald.
LB2831.92.F57   1995
371.2′012′0973—dc20   95-22960
                                                                            CIP

Editor: Cheryl Kimball
Production: J.B. Tranchemontagne
Cover design: Jenny Jensen Greenleaf

Printed in the United States of America on acid-free paper
99 98   VB   2   3   4   5   6   7   8   9

To Be of Use

The people I love the best
jump into work head first
without dallying in the shallows
and swim off with sure strokes almost out of sight.
They seem to become natives of that element,
the black sleek heads of seals
bouncing like half-submerged balls.

I love people who harness themselves, an ox to a heavy cart,
who pull like water buffalo, with massive patience,
who strain in the mud and the muck to move things forward,
who do what has to be done, again and again.

I want to be with people who submerge
in a task, who go into the fields to harvest
and work in a row and pass the bags along,
who are not parlor generals and field deserters
and move in a common rhythm
when the food must come in or the fire be put out.

The work of the world is common as mud.
Botched, it smears the hands, crumbles to dust.
But the thing worth doing well done
has a shape that satisfies, clean and evident.
Greek amphoras for wine or oil,
Hopi vases that held corn, are put in museums
but you know they were made to be used.
The pitcher cries for water to carry
and a person for work that is real.

Marge Piercy

Contents

Foreword

YOU ARE ABOUT TO ENTER THE PERSONAL AND PROFES-
sional lives of thirty remarkable educators. The stories they tell
here are as varied as the actors themselves who have played on the
stages of public and private, elementary, middle, and high, wealthy
and impoverished schools around the country. Yet all of these
authors have in common two distinctive qualities: each was once a
beginning school head, and each has chosen to share with us in
writing that turbulent first year.

The language in these sometimes poetic accounts reveals the
delight, the frustration, and above all the ambiguity attendant to
that initial year. The words with which these formative experiences are wrapped move me deeply for they evoke my own unfor-
gettable first year as principal of an inner-city school. Indeed, the
paradoxes and passions that jump out of these pages are generic,
common to everyone's beginning experience as an educator:

> wonderful and wicked
> control and chaos
> hugs and heartaches
> isolation and collegiality
> respected and unloved
> power and powerlessness
> conviction and compromise
> prosecutor and jury
> leadership and luck

pleasure and adversity
confidence and self-doubt
tenacity and vulnerability
firmness and flexibility
work and play
faith and fear
humor and pathos
stability and change
surprise and routinization.

But what shines through these accounts for me, above all, is the profound and often painful learning of the novice school leader. The learning curves of these educators are steep indeed. As one put it, "Nothing could have prepared me for my first year as principal." And another, "But once in the principal's office my true education had just begun."

In the pages that follow, you, too, will learn what each of these school heads learned. You will go where they went and sit with them in their offices that sometimes resemble a courtroom, sometimes a seminar, sometimes a board meeting, and most often a hospital emergency ward.

It is an all too common belief that when a school practitioner speaks, what emerges is a "war story." Indeed, I find many vivid descriptions of practice do resemble war stories. But when these portrayals of practice are accompanied by careful and thoughtful analysis and reflection, as they are here, war stories are transformed into abundant craft knowledge. This collection offers a fine-grained description and analysis of one year in the past—with important lessons for the future. The wisdom of the craft revealed here has much to offer those who aspire to be principals and those who aspire to prepare others for the principalship and, of course, those who are themselves experiencing their first year as head of a school. Whatever stereotypes one holds about school leaders—whether as heroic commander on a white horse or as innocuous manager pushing papers—are likely to be updated, perhaps violated, by these vivid portraits.

I found myself unable to read through this volume continuously. Rather, I find these little vignettes best consumed, like peanuts, a few at a time, allowing plenty of opportunity to savor and chew them over. "Have you got a minute?" are words heard frequently by heads of schools. When I heard them, I never knew what was coming next. If you do have a minute, you are in for an unusual journey in the unexpected world of the beginning school leader. Part of the surprise for me was discovering that I had worked with and for many of these authors over the years. I think all of us will discover here some unexpected connections with our past.

One of the great paradoxes of school life is that elementary, middle, and high schools are thought to be places that promote the learning of young people. These stories suggest just how much the schoolhouse can be a rich context for the development of educators themselves. Powerful, replenishing learning comes to those who reflect on practice—and to those of us who are privy to their reflections.

Roland S. Barth

Preface

I<small>N</small> S<small>EPTEMBER</small> 1991, S<small>COTT</small> M<small>C</small>V<small>AY</small>, <small>EXECUTIVE</small> director of the Geraldine R. Dodge Foundation, and I met with the directors of four principals' centers. As Millie Blackman, Michael Gillespie, India Podsen, and Laverne Scott spoke to us about their experiences with principals, I passed Scott a note which said, "What about doing a book called *First Year as Principal?*" Scott smiled, since the idea proceeded naturally from Dodge Foundation support of a prior book, *The First Year of Teaching* (Walker 1991).

The Dodge Foundation had been looking at the role of principal in the complex ecosystem of schools for some time. With long experience in making grants directed to secondary schools and more recently to middle and elementary schools, the foundation was ready to launch a major initiative seeking to promote principals as "instructional leaders," a phrase that is connected to the original role that school leaders played.

Over the last half century, as central office bureaucracy has grown to meet new demands (and created some demands of its own), the job of the principal has changed. Whereas once the "educational buck" might have stopped at the principal's office in all matters relating directly to the classroom, in many schools the role of principal is no longer that of academic catalyst or explorer of new possibilities for teaching and learning. People involved with schools (and certainly many parents) wonder where the leadership is in education because all too often those who have, or

xv

appear to have, the authority and responsibility are not in the school-house itself.

For all the national lament about the quality of schools, there are, of course, some stunning exceptions that give hope for the future. And where these exceptions are found, typically we also find a principal who is a true instructional leader, an educator whose vision stays focused on the full potential of schools and whose eyes betray the joy of learning no matter how persistent the distractions. This book is an effort to let principals share their own stories with those who are considering a career in school leadership and also with the general public—both policymakers and the polity—who need to understand better what school leadership requires.

To find these stories, the foundation advertised nationally, calling for essays that shed light on the "human side" of school leadership especially as it is experienced during that first critical year on the job. Responses came from people who had led every type of school in almost every state (and Canada). Some of these principals were looking back as far as forty years; a few took pen (or rather word processor) in hand literally as they were completing their first year. Each essay was reviewed by five experienced school leaders who took on the difficult task of ranking. This book contains the top thirty essays from that process.

The stories share at least two themes, one of which is the basic realization that the step into the principal's office has a significantly higher rise than the smooth progression of treads preceding it. Here we find career educators who have spent years in the classroom working with students, colleagues, and parents and who by all accounts know the essence of schooling as well as the technical side of how school "keeps." Yet, pulling it all together and providing the vision of where a school ought to go next require a whole new set of skills. Leadership, it appears, is not experienced by the leader in quite the way it is experienced by those being led.

A second theme is the frustration felt by many principals who set out to provide instructional leadership for their schools but soon find themselves in a dozen other roles ranging from traffic cop to plumber, fire fighter to arbitrator. Leadership means knowing what to do when the country is shocked by the assassination of its president, or when it ought to be more shocked by the tragedy of how it treats even one of its children. But it means other things, too—like going through the trash looking for a child's lost dime-store ring, encouraging a bull to leave the school yard, or being on the "gotcha" end of a practical joke cooked up by two playful teachers. The challenge is finding the balance or the variety of balances needed to meet the myriad needs of every student and every teacher under conditions that are mostly unpredictable and often uncontrollable.

The essays begin with a journal entry from Johanna VanderMolen, who gives us a Vermeer-like peek into the daily life of a first-year principal. They end with a pair of stories written by Joseph and Mark Segar, father and son, each of whom followed his own path to the principal's office. In the middle are twenty-seven others by a fascinating array of educators. These stories pertain only to the people who wrote them. Yet taken together, they tell a broader story that in one way or another has something to say to every school leader and to all who care about schools.

In my work as editor and midwife for this book, I have many people to thank. Cheryl Kimball at Heinemann has been there every step of the way coaxing, guiding, offering good suggestions—always in a gentle way. Her predecessor at Heinemann, Tom Seavey, saw the Dodge Foundation's "Call for Essays" and thought the book was such a good idea that he contacted us to see if we had a publisher. While such an approach makes good business sense for a publisher, the folks at Heinemann care first about schools, and I believe Tom's call had much more to do with good education than good business. Also, Gail Gorman, my assistant at Cambridge College, has done yeoman service keeping all the strands of this project from unraveling.

Roland Barth has been a spiritual guide long before the idea for this book came onto anyone's screen. Not only is he the godfather of perhaps *every* center for principals in the country, but his clear vision about the way schools can and should work has helped many educators. In his Foreword we get to hear his overview of how these stories fit with the insights he has gained from his distinguished career working with principals.

Also, to Scott McVay, the Dodge trustees, and my wonderful colleagues at the foundation, I am deeply grateful for a spirit that is difficult to capture in words. The foundation operates with a level of hope and passion that I have never experienced any other place. It was a joy to spend long days at 163 Madison Avenue and to know the many people whose lives and dreams intersect with the foundation. Scott McVay's Introduction to this volume provides a window into his own personal commitment to education and his faith in people. He was the one who suggested we include Marge Piercy's "To Be of Use" and that we use Lonni Sue Johnson's drawing for the cover. Together they tell quite a story. Although Scott has never held the title "teacher," he is one of the best I ever had.

Finally, I am grateful for the support of my family, especially my wife, Joanne Hoffman, who started her own first year as a school head while this book was being edited and produced. On many early mornings and late nights, I would hear her worrying over the very same challenges I was reading about in the essays scattered across my desk. Her experience was all the proof I needed to confirm the validity of these stories.

In the end, the purpose of schooling is to make sure that all children have the chance to know themselves and to explore the world with the vision and gifts that are theirs alone. People who want to lead schools know that, and their singular goal, often against great odds, is to serve those children well. For me, the purpose of schools and this book is intensely personal: I wish for my daughter, Katie, and for my stepdaughter, Caitlin, that every school always be as good as its promise. We can tolerate nothing less.

Ronald Thorpe

Among a Company of Pilgrims

EARLY IN THE CENTURY NOW DRAWING TO A CLOSE, George Ade was writing pieces known as fables for a newspaper in the Midwest. He had a great following. Readers were hungry for what he dished up almost daily, and the fables answered a need in people's lives the way a good story or poem might. His fables were more read than Aesop's in those parts.

My favorite is "The Old Fox and the Young Fox." One day Old Fox called in Young Fox to share with him a few hard-won nuggets of truth gleaned from having spent some time in this valley. Young Fox yawned since he knew things the way a sophomore knows things. His eyes glazed over as he tuned out. Yet in that little fable are hints and clues about how to live that don't compete with the Ten Commandments but nonetheless contain some practical stuff.

For instance, one of Old Fox's maxims is, "Never accuse a Man of being Lazy. There is no such thing as Laziness. If a Man does not go about his work with Enthusiasm, it means that he has not yet found . . . the Task that Destiny has set aside for him."

Or, notes the Old Fox, "An Ounce of Prevention is worth a Pound of Cure and costs more. Don't attempt to prevent Trouble or you will lose your eyesight watching so many corners at the same time. Wait until Trouble comes and then consult a Specialist." Or, "If you expect to be a popular After-Dinner Speaker, don't attempt to work at anything else. That is a sufficiently large contract for one brief Existence."

The book you hold in your hands is a first attempt to gather in one place the experience of the first year as a principal. You will read here that prior schooling and experience as a teacher do not fully prepare anyone for that daunting first year, a year that can almost overwhelm the vision of the first day.

But the spirit and generosity of these thirty essays suggest that if teaching is one of the highest callings to which a human being can aspire, then to be the principal teacher or lead learner must be the absolute fulcrum of school reform.

Written from many points on the trajectory of experience, from the vantage point of a retired principal recalling that vivid first year to one who has been one year in the saddle, each essay sheds light on the extraordinary opportunity to be a good principal. Fables abound as do "morals of the fables." Ade suggests, "Even the Elders can give a number of Helpful Hints."

This book is meant for any principal or aspiring principal, but we expect that it will be most closely read by those new at the craft or considering it closely. Their antennae are out, and they may already be dealing with the flywheel of daily events in a large community of children and adults. And they (you) will find instruction and solace in the thoughts of those who are just ahead on the path of instructional leadership.

Who will not read closely Barbara Landis Chase's "The Best News of All" that sees the first year as crucible. As she looks back on the first year, the lessons she came to understand and believe remain valid. So many points jump out, seem honest and helpful, including:

> It is hard for others to comprehend the power of the connection we feel to our schools. I know that this was something I never understood until I walked this ground.

And a thought can animate a school and drive the vision of that learning community:

> My own litmus test for every decision is to ask if it is the right thing for the students: present and future.

At a Celebration of Teaching event in 1992 honoring the County Teachers of the Year in New Jersey, four recipients spoke of breakthrough strategies in teaching. In each case they felt that had they asked permission, it would have been denied, and yet those very ideas were what won them acclaim. As Mary Ann Sinkkonen notes:

> The best advice I received as I was beginning that first year was, "Use your position to say, 'Yes.'"

In Albert Adams's fascinating piece, wherein he met in the early days of his principalship with parents, teachers, students, and alumni, he made a good map of the territory of that school. In identifying the themes that define his school, including challenges that require attention, he notes:

> In many cases it is recurring stories, rather than specific information, which provide the deepest insights.

Here, too, you will find recurring stories, some familiar, others surprisingly fresh, yet speaking to your precise situation. As a principal, new or seasoned, you will see that your triumphs and travails are widely shared. Those of you who had a tough but exhilarating first year will find here others who fared less well.

But, overall, you will be left with the impression that you are among a company of pilgrims on a quest to make vibrant communities of learners. You are learning by doing, swapping stories along the way, and reconfirming at every step the initial tug to teaching that has shaped your lifework.

Scott McVay

Then and Now: Lessons of a New Principal

JOHANNA A. VANDERMOLEN

JOURNAL ENTRY, JUNE 12, 1988

As the sun comes up tomorrow morning I'll hurry across town to finish my first year as an elementary school principal. But sleep does not close my eyes tonight although the stars are out and the evening is late and cool. Before me I see student faces who will move on to middle school, faces that laughed *at* me and *with* me, those who cried when I counseled them, and others who begged me to give them another chance before I called mom or dad to let them know that their child had broken some school rule. I see Jeanne who confided to me that she had been sexually assaulted by a neighbor since attending the third grade, and Carlos who used pictures to communicate because his desire to speak was abruptly taken away by insufferable traumas no child should have to endure. And prideful Joey, who is so rough and tough, always looking for a fight, and who, just as often, has sat in my office and cried for his long-lost father. I'm going to miss them deeply, for they have indeed touched and changed my life.

I have felt sadness, exasperation, challenges, joy, and frustration this year. I have also learned about humankind, forgiveness, hardships, working with people, and building working relationships. My heart has ached and bled, but mostly it sang with jubilation at the love that I saw teachers give to children every day.

These teachers and the parents of the children with whom I have worked have been supportive, challenging, and stimulating. They have also at times been unmoving and difficult.

1

My first job as principal began late one Wednesday evening in February 1988 when I received a phone call from the superintendent requesting that I take an elementary principalship the following Monday morning. As a middle school assistant principal, I had my back pocket stuffed with years of elementary experience, so I agreed. I fumbled my way through the week closing out my current job and on Monday drove across town to my new assignment.

Nothing could have prepared me for my first year as principal. The school I entered was overcrowded and experiencing boundary changes that were opposed by both the teachers and the parents. As a result, the faculty was depressed and the parents were angry.

I knew little about the situation, the anger, or the depression before I became the school's principal. This, in retrospect, was probably my saving grace. I simply accepted the school as a new, exciting experience and assumed that everyone wanted to work together in harmony.

I had believed that when I became a principal I would be a notable instructional leader. This school was so demoralized, however, that at the end of a few weeks I decided to place my job as instructional leader on hold and focus on a more immediate concern: staff and community morale.

Fortunately, this faculty was one of the best with which I had ever worked—energetic, professional, and, as I found out later that year, very enthusiastic. They were a great group of people to whom I was drawn both professionally and personally. We established a tennis club where many faculty members took tennis lessons together (I can freely admit that I was the worst player) and a monthly Literature Club. Many of us repainted the faculty room during that first summer.

JOURNAL ENTRY, JUNE 1993:

It's five years later, and I've just reread my journal from that first year. It makes me sit back, reflect, and smile. Over the course of that year the boundary changes were made and, contrary to the fears of the staff and community, the school continued to be successful, earning the California Distinguished School Award the following year.

I'm still a principal but in a different school and city. In reflection I recognize that many of my current "guiding principles" were initially developed during that first year:

· Choose Your Battles
I learned to prioritize what needed to be done. I had to realize that I could NOT do everything at once and that some problems are just more pressing than others.

- Stay Focused
  I learned to decide what my goals are and then make decisions throughout the year supporting those goals. By staying focused I have found that I can get more done without being scattered in many directions.
- Build Upon the Successes the School Already Has
  I learned that teachers and parents take enormous pride in their school, even if there are problems. By building upon the actual and perceived successes of the school, I have found that changes can be made.
- Keep Things in Perspective
  I learned that friends and mentors are to be cherished, for through discussions with these people the perceived vastness of many problems will diminish.

I now visualize the course of a school as a river with smooth currents and pounding, steep rapids. My school sits upon this river, moving with the flow. Empowered by my "guiding principles," there are rapids that I choose to run and those that are best to circumvent. There are smooth waters that are comfortable, but when the calm continues too long, I can lift my oar, stir the current, and challenge the crew to explore new territory. Most important, I must keep us all flowing toward our main goal—discovering what is in the best interest of our children.

JOHANNA VANDERMOLEN IS THE PRINCIPAL OF THE NORTHWOOD SCHOOL IN NAPA, CALIFORNIA.

The Best News of All

BARBARA LANDIS CHASE

Slowly, I place the thirteenth standard black "Day-At-A-Glance" at the end of the line with its twelve identical partners standing on the bottom bookshelf in my office. My first impulse is to turn away immediately, giving my attention to the crisp, new 1993–94 academic planner sitting at the ready on my desk across the room. But a vague sense of wistfulness holds me back, as it has every year when I have performed this entirely private but somehow momentous ritual. Glancing down this row of silent chroniclers of my years as a school head, I look at the first book and think back to the young woman who had so much to learn in that first year.

I started that year with a bag of tricks and a Pandora's box, not of evils, but of inexperience. On one hand, I was generally, at least as far as I could tell, a candidate with whom people at the school were satisfied. I was young (thirty-five) and energetic. I had, for whatever reason, the confidence that I could do a good job. My husband was enormously supportive. This all-girl school was strong and established; the board savvy and eager to be helpful.

On the other hand, I was deficient in many areas: I had almost no experience in finance or development, writing for publication, or public speaking. Yet I would have to work with a multi-million dollar budget, raise money, write a monthly column for the school newsletter, and speak to countless student assemblies and parent and alumnae meetings. I had not hired, fired, or supervised anyone in my previous experience as teacher and then as director of admission, but in that first year, I would need to make a number of very tough personnel decisions.

4

I can't honestly say I learned everything I know about independent school leadership in that first year; I must have known a little bit going into it. Certainly I have learned a lot since. Even more certainly, I still have much to learn. The first year of any experience is, in many ways, a crucible. You reveal the way you think and understand the world. You set patterns of behavior that henceforth become expectations. You settle pretty substantially the issue of trust.

What did the events of that first year teach me about leadership—a subject heretofore theoretical and secondhand but now so real and so personal? Looking back, I can see that the lessons I came to understand and believe that first year have remained valid for me. The events of subsequent years have fleshed them out, given them new and fascinating faces, but have never changed them. The ambiguity that is a condition of life for school heads means that every rule has its important exception and that embedded in every axiom is the undoing of the axiomatic. Nevertheless, I believe it is important for me to hold to these lessons. I can't say how valid they are for other people in other schools. Maybe what is most important is for each of us to sit down every once in a while and take the time to consider what these lessons are for us. Here are mine:

LESSON 1

You must learn to live with frustration; the multitudinous demands of the job are such that you will constantly disappoint people—including yourself.

This is a job, I am fond of saying, for people with short attention spans. We never do one thing long enough to become bored. That is the good news. The bad news is that we are pulled in so many directions that we rarely feel satisfied that we have truly finished one thing. Just dealing with the mail is daunting. In my first year, I went through the mail every day and sorted out the things I needed to deal with right then and there. I put everything else onto a "reading pile" on a shelf by my desk. At the beginning of the summer, I began going through the pile, and I discovered many things that I really should have done something about earlier: announcements of important professional development opportunities, articles that could have informed talks, and articles I had to turn out. But I simply couldn't deal with all the paper. I've learned to cope with the flood of paper much more expeditiously—yet the reading pile still mounts up as the busy spring accelerates toward graduation. We do see some absolutely fascinating and sometimes very inspiring reading cross our desks: from the latest issue of the *Harvard Education Review* to letters of gratitude from recent or not-so-recent graduates. We are lucky, as school heads, to have a change of pace in the summer—allowing us to catch up on important and enriching reading.

The mail represents only a small fraction of the time demands. Daily, hourly, minute by minute, we try to meet the needs and expectations of the people who comprise the major constituencies we serve: students, faculty, parents, alumnae, trustees, the community. They each have their own needs and they can't possibly all be met because of time restraints and because the needs of various constituencies are often in conflict. As independent school heads, we are the chief executive officers of small businesses (non-profit though they be), but we are also the head teachers.

Beyond the routine administrative matters, we are called upon to handle, competently, any unusual events. In that first year, I had to hire a new business manager midyear, and then I had to work with that new business manager to cope with the situation when our food service manager quit on very short notice. As I recall, between us we figured out how many loaves of bread and how much peanut butter and jelly we would need to go out and buy, if it came to that. What did any of this have to do with academics? Not much. But at the same time, I was learning to recognize the strengths and weaknesses of each faculty member, the rationale for the science sequence, and the need for a major revision of the advising program.

I learned that the trustees and parents expected me to run the school like a well-run business but also to know them and their children and each faculty member personally and to be accessible in person or by telephone, whether at 7:30 A.M. or 7:30 P.M. I was expected to keep up with the administrative side of things and also to appear at each hockey game, the Upper School performance of "Oklahoma," and parent meetings for every division of the school. The students wanted a headmistress they could feel close to, that is, spend time with, and the development director wanted me to get out on the road to meet the alumnae. Finally, I learned that fulfilling all of these expectations was absolutely impossible and thus, that I would be disappointing people, including myself, all of the time. I also learned that I derived surprising pleasure and real energy from coming into contact with all of these people in so many settings. I almost always felt energized and enthusiastic about what I was doing and the work the school was doing after one of these events. Often, it was pure fun.

LESSON 2

Be willing to do the right thing and then live with the sudden silence in the faculty room when you walk in. And, as a corollary: Learn to reach out to your colleagues.

Ours is often a lonely job. The hard decisions are most often ours to make. You can't please all of the people in any given situation, even if that is precisely what you set out to do, so you might as well try to do the right thing, even if it doesn't win you popularity in the short run. My own litmus test for every decision is to ask if it is the right thing for the students: present and future. They are the only reason we exist. That first year, I discovered that the faculty were permitted to smoke in the lunchroom—a practice I decided should end. At an early faculty meeting, I simply told them they couldn't—by edict or fiat or whatever you might wish to call such an authoritarian move. They accepted it—some, rather reluctantly. Yet, I sensed that I had only a certain number of chips to use up this way. Most decisions were much more participatory.

Doing what is right for students doesn't mean doing just what they would have you do. That first year, I needed to tighten up on rules for dances. It was not a popular move, and the students let me know it. So I learned to accept and live with the feeling of being unloved.

And I learned the important need for political grounding. The board of trustees had better be ready to support you, which means they had better know what you're about and understand and agree with it. Most of all, they had better not be unhappily surprised. It is, after all, the board who hired you, and it is they who have the power to fire you if they don't think you are doing a good job. There were and continue to be too many examples of heads losing their jobs because they have lost the support of the board.

And now for the corollary: I also learned the critical importance of the telephone as lifeline when times get tough and life feels lonely. The only people who completely understand what you are going through are the people who have gone through it themselves: other school heads. I learned to call the colleagues I trust and admire and seek their advice and sympathy. I have never called and been rebuffed. I have never hung up and not felt better.

LESSON 3

Learn from your mistakes; learn to know yourself as other people perceive you. Then try to change the things you can change and live with the things you can't.

I learned this lesson the first time I got back the results of formal evaluations from the board and faculty. They said some very nice things. People seemed to think I was doing a good job—but, of course, not a perfect one.

The most frustrating thing was that it was hard to respond to the negative feedback. Evidently, some people found me *too* efficient and (I'll never forget this particular phrase) "not the warmest person in the world." At first, I was devastated. *I* knew I was a warm, emotional, *personal* kind of person. The feedback just had to be wrong. But the more I thought and talked about it with people I knew and trusted, the more philosophical I became. It was true that I could become so immersed in an issue or problem that I might seem aloof or distant. This tendency became clear one day as I was walking across campus with something on my mind and suddenly realized that I had passed two people without saying hello. On another occasion, a trustee I looked up to and trusted was kind enough to tell me that, although she knew I didn't do it deliberately, I sometimes rolled my eyes in meetings when things were proceeding too slowly or people were being obtuse. So, I learned there was some truth in the perception.

But I also came to believe, and still do, that women have a particularly difficult time in positions like ours. We are expected to be efficient in our executive duties, and we are also criticized for seeming *too* businesslike, *too* professional. In short, we can't win. I have learned to accept this as a paradox of our current evolving gender attitudes, but I cannot stress enough the importance of seeking and using self-knowledge, informed by an understanding of how others see us. We *must* learn from our mistakes. And our most important mistakes (and, thus our most important opportunities for victories) come in the area of human relations.

LESSON 4

Hire the very best administrators you can find. Then stand back and let them do their jobs. Support them assiduously. Accept the blame for things that go wrong and give them the credit for everything that goes right.

I learned quickly that the people with whom I worked most closely every day were extremely important to me. They needed my ear for listening and my arm for support, and I needed them to make sure things went well. I couldn't possibly do everything myself. I had to be ready to help them solve a tricky personnel problem or talk through a challenging situation with a student. I needed to praise them freely and give them constructive criticism. I needed to support their professional growth and development, even when it meant helping them to move on to another position and thus losing them. I owe this not only to them, but to the profession. In short, I learned that the power I had as head of the school was exponentially enhanced if I shared it with these people. The more I enabled and empowered them, the more got done, the more progress we made.

LESSON 5

Come to understand the nature of your connection with the school as its leader. Learn to use it, but always understand the underlying danger of its power.

I have thought about this paradox so much that I have given it a strange name: "Materfamilias and Jonah's Whale." It is hard for others to comprehend the power of the connection we feel to our schools. I know that this was something I never understood until I walked this ground. We are, whether we want to be or not, in a real sense the mothers or fathers of these school families. When there is crisis, we feel the stress of full responsibility. The bomb threat or fire or lawsuit rests on our shoulders far more heavily than on anyone else's. When there is loss, we grieve and yet must be strong for everyone, just like parents in any family. I learned early how important it is for the leader to be on the scene, visible and strong in these inevitable times of crisis, or celebration, or ritual, or loss—how important it is to say the right things in a moving way, to shepherd the community safely through these passages.

I also began to notice, almost from the beginning, that although this connection was intensely beautiful and meaningful, it was also dangerous. As school heads, we are all tempted to think of and speak of these schools as "ours." Many of us use the personal possessive "my" before "faculty" or "school." We do this at our peril. These are institutions far beyond our illusory power to shape or guide them. Our school was founded a hundred years before I came onto the scene, and it will prevail long after I am gone. My stewardship, although important, was not all-important. Calling the school "my school" would be like Jonah calling the whale that had swallowed him up, carried him for three days and three nights through the sea, "my whale." The institutions we lead carry us to lands we could never have imagined, on a course we chart with limited proficiency.

I came to believe that this sense of connection the leader feels for the institution she leads had better be tempered with a large grain of humility. I came to believe this after seeing several school heads, who had spent years at an institution, forced to leave not on their own terms but terminated, fired, or, as the euphemism has come to be used, "disruptively separated" at great cost to themselves and the school. They and the school were not, after all, one and the same. And that is a good thing, if only we can remember it. We need to be separate from our institutions, not only because it is good for them, but because it is the only way for us to maintain our own mental health. Having what our students would call "a life" (as in "Get one!") is absolutely essential.

I reflect, as I turn from the shelf with my thirteen years lined up on it, that for all its frustrations and riskiness, I cannot think of a job I would rather be doing. What we do as school heads matters—really matters. Working in a place that cares about and educates young people stimulates us, challenges us, gratifies us. That line of thirteen books represents one of the best things about life as a school head: each year we get a fresh chance to start all over again. Each September brings a new opportunity to get on a new footing with all of those myriad constituencies. We get to give another talk at parents' evenings, work with a new senior class, write another Class Day Talk, forge a stronger relationship with each of our colleagues. The best news of all is that we will never do it perfectly, so we have the chance each year to try again to do it a little better.

BARBARA LANDIS CHASE IS HEAD OF SCHOOL AT PHILLIPS ACADEMY IN ANDOVER, MASSACHUSETTS.

There's Nothing As Practical As a Good Theory

SARAH L. LEVINE

This piece is about the confluence of theories, desires, and realities during my first year as head of a small elementary school. With the perspective of subsequent years, it is also about the importance of conviction, tenacity, flexibility, humility, and patience.

W hen I walked into my office on that steamy July morning, feelings of fear far outweighed the confidence I had exuded during the search process. Certainly I knew a lot about leading schools; I had been sharing the latest research with principals and other school leaders around the country for the last six years in my job at the Harvard Principals' Center. Yet for all the time I had spent in schools and for the many times I stood in front of principals, heads, superintendents, and even state commissioners, I had never actually sat in their chairs or walked in their shoes in the offices and schools where the real and complex issues of school leadership come to rest.

What I brought to the principalship was a set of theories—convictions—about: schools as communities of learners and leaders; writing as a powerful tool for staff development; practice shaped by core values; and adult growth as a fundamental condition for children's development. With all the idealism of a first-year principal tempered by the realities of a mid-life adult, I wanted to share with children, teachers, and parents my convictions and commitments so that together we could bring to life the possibilities and promises that reside within every school.

Soon after my appointment, I learned that for some members of the hiring committee, offering the role of head to someone from a university was a mighty leap of faith. Why would a person want to move from "higher" to "lower" education? Would I be aloof, impractical, or overly academic? Rather than an asset, my affiliation with Harvard was something I needed to overcome. Manifestations of this consideration came from both parents and faculty. During my first weeks, I sent parents an article by a well-known early childhood educator. While I didn't agree with all that the article proposed, I thought the ideas were provocative and might lead to interesting discussion. Immediately, the article and my views became synonymous. Sharing research only fanned the fires for those worried about the new head's overly academic frame of reference.

Determined to make faculty meetings substantive, I spoke to teachers about school culture during opening school meetings, modifying a talk I had given successfully many times before—complete with overheads! "We're not in graduate school," I heard within minutes of completing the presentation. This was neither the first nor final time I was to feel a keen sense of uneasiness when what I believed to be important was not immediately embraced.

I have a firm belief in writing as a tool for staff development. This belief was generated and nurtured at the Principals' Center, and principals who came there for the summer couldn't wait to return to their schools, journals in hand. So what if they later told me it was hard to keep up the practice once the school year began? So what if they could never convince their faculties of the power and importance of writing? It would be a different story for *me* with *my* teachers. Of that I was (almost) certain.

"I'd like to tell you about 'freewriting'," I said enthusiastically at the beginning of a faculty meeting. "Freewriting is putting pen to paper and continuing to write whatever comes to mind without stopping. If you get stuck, just write 'I'm stuck, I'm stuck, I'm stuck' until your next thought comes." During the first year, I asked faculty and staff to bring to every meeting the journals I had given each of them. Before we talked about a complex issue— children and discipline, or faculty evaluation—I asked everyone, myself included, to freewrite about it.

The first few times, everyone wrote. Then some wrote while others stared out toward the playground. "Oh, were we supposed to bring our journals?" asked two teachers almost at the same time. It seems both had left their writing notebooks back in their classrooms. Again that uneasy feeling made its way up and down my spine. Was this to be another potent theory without practical meaning? Almost always our discussions were enriched by our written reflections. Yet, some teachers felt the writing and talking took time and energy away from the *doing*. Together we are still searching for a comfortable balance.

Establishing core values and creating a common vision—these tenets I *knew* to be as valid in practice as they are in the ivy-covered towers of academe. Convinced of this wisdom, I asked the art teacher to cover the bulletin boards at the school's entrance with these three statements: Everyone Can Learn; Celebrate Diversity; and BDS (our school initials) Means Community. Indisputable values, I thought confidently, and ones that everyone could get behind. Long discussions and debates about the multiple meanings of diversity or the strengths and limits of school as community have since complicated my thinking. Nevertheless I have appreciated and learned from the open and honest interchange that has helped us move toward common ground.

Everyone Can Learn—simple enough, I thought, and certainly beyond question. "What promises are we making when we say everyone can learn?" a veteran teacher asked seriously soon after the brightly colored letters appeared. "Are we saying that the school will find a way to reach every child? What if a child has insurmountable limitations?" At almost the same moment, we recalled a recent legal case where a nearby school was backpedaling from such a claim. Putting core values on a bulletin board in bright letters was clearly easier than defining them, putting them into practice, or defending them.

Finally, I brought to my new school a belief in the importance of adult development as a *prerequisite* for children's growth. Teachers must feel vital and alive about their work in order for students to be engaged in meaningful and sustained learning. To think about schools as communities of learners where everyone—children, teachers, principal, and parents—is learning was a new and not-so-obvious idea for some. After all, elementary and secondary schools are for children and adolescents. Since when did adults factor into the equation?

Commensurate with the high value I place upon adult growth, one of the first things I asked from my board was an allocation of substantial funds for professional development. But finding good substitute teachers is not always easy, and children need consistency in the classroom. What about those times when funds are limited, and hard decisions have to be made about their allocation? Since schools must take account of diverse perspectives, I now hold my thinking about adult growth in a broader context of substitutes, consistency for children, and making hard choices with limited funds. Decisions in practice are not always as simple as theory would make them seem. Now, when the dailiness of school life dampens my idealism, it is teachers who remind me how important it is for them to grow *so that* their students can learn.

Why share all of this as a reflection on the first year of the principalship? Why not offer a story or vignette that captures a more finite aspect of how I have come to make sense of school leadership? I choose to paint a broader picture for several reasons. Many of the issues I have written about that seemed so new, so hard, and so unsettling during my first year have, with considerable persistence, patience, and a willingness to learn, become "the way we do things around here" at the school. Rather than abnormalities to be questioned, they are norms increasingly valued if still to be explained, examined, and refined.

Not every one of the beliefs or theories I brought with me has proved resilient or even relevant to the particular school culture I inherited and have now helped to shape. But many *have* become meaningful, and others that originated from faculty, staff, parents, and children have contributed to my growth and to the school's collective vision. All along I have been grateful for the theories and perspectives I brought with me and for the views about schools, school leadership, and children's learning that others have contributed to the continuing conversation.

What really happened to me that first year as a principal and every year since is that I have brought my views and theories into the school as clearly and forcefully as I believe them. I also have worked to keep myself open to new ideas, and especially to ideas that are different from mine. Gradually, I am learning to tolerate that uneasy feeling that still runs up and down my spine when I encounter differences and disagreements. But I can't think of a better or more important place to make theory good and practical nor a place where I would rather work and learn.

Most principals will agree that children tend to accept new ideas more quickly than do many adults. At the end of my first year, several fifth graders presented me with a wooden plaque they had been crafting together for months in the shop. Choosing an assembly where the impact of the gift would be most widely evident, they ceremoniously handed me the sign, which reads: HEAD LEARNER. With their help, I hung it near the top of my office door— just to be sure that I, and all the adults who pass by, cannot help but read it!

SARAH L. LEVINE IS HEAD AT THE BELMONT DAY SCHOOL IN BELMONT, MASSACHUSETTS.

Detective, Prosecutor, Judge, and Jury

GORDON A. DONALDSON, JR.

"Just sit down and shut your mouth, Jason! . . . Now, Carol, where were you yesterday fourth period, Ms. Stark has you marked absent? . . . Aw, come on, Carol, you said you were in Clinic *last* week, too. Are you sick or just sick of Civics?" So began another day for me at Ellsworth Junior-Senior High School in Ellsworth, Maine. In 1976, at the age of thirty, I became principal of EJSHS, a school of eight hundred students, grades 7–12.

Each day began with a parade of students who were called to the office for various infractions the previous day. My job was to stand on the "other side" of the office counter, question the twenty to thirty students who had been summoned on the public address system about their infractions, and mete out punishments. It was the linchpin of a system of discipline I inherited. I suspect it had been developed because it beat chasing kids all day and pulling them out of classes to interrogate them. Once I got the hang of it, the system seemed to work well—as long as I ignored some fundamental principles of human decency.

In retrospect, I am embarrassed by the insensitivity I showed toward students. "Sit down and shut your mouth, Jason!" was the only way I could deflect a protesting sixteen-year-old so that I could get to the other twenty students who were waiting "their turn" at the counter (and enjoying Jason's performance at my expense!). Calling Carol's "sickness" into question in public put her on the defensive and allowed me to cut to the chase with a minimum of dialogue—again because I had so many kids waiting and missing their first-period classes.

The principal's insensitivity, though, came with the system. The role required me to be a modern-day Inquisitor. With ominous voice, I called students to the office over the public address system. They (usually) showed up dutifully, milling around the office door until I summoned each one to the counter. There, each received his or her minute of public grilling from me as I tried to get to "the bottom" of his or her misdemeanor. If time and I permitted, a student could explain his or her "side." At the conclusion, I would declare an end to the "fact-finding" and often issue a punishment to fit the crime. I was detective, prosecutor, judge, *and* jury all in one. And I did it all in one minute per case! I participated in this judicial charade for two years before I had the courage to change it.

Changing it was difficult because this traditional system served some institutional—and some personal—purposes. Public lists of student names boomed through the classrooms of the school serving notice to all that Donaldson was ever-vigilant! Nobody escaped the daily dragnet for class-skippers and transgressors of minor rules. (Of course, major violations were handled instantaneously!) The public grilling at "the counter" added a touch of public shaming to the process: you were presumed guilty by virtue of being called to the office; now you had to defend yourself on this very exposed village green. Finally, Donaldson would announce the punishment, serving notice to all that, yes, discipline was strong at EJSHS.

The system I inherited was, as well, successful in establishing and sustaining my own position as a disciplinarian. As a relatively young principal who was entirely new to such a big school, I knew I had to "earn my spurs" in the eyes of faculty, staff, and community. The "public-ness" of the traditional system for routine discipline put me on display. My remarks to Jason and Carol, uttered with appropriate sternness, said to everyone: "Donaldson's no pushover." The more adept I got at pinning kids down on their stories in a short period of time, the more the students would see that "you can't get away with anything with Donaldson."

But the system was wrong. It *did* work for the institution by nabbing miscreants and helping to maintain order. And it *did* work for me by reinforcing my power as a disciplinarian and my control over the system. But it mistreated kids. And in a way it mistreated me. It violated the basic purpose of a school to help youngsters develop a sense of justice and respect for themselves and for others.

I began to realize this about five months into the job, only after I had made the system work. The school was running fine. Faculty and students pretty much did what they were supposed to. Major disciplinary events did not disrupt the school but, oddly, the stream of minor violations leading to the morning Inquisition had not diminished. When, I wondered, were these kids going to stop skipping classes and committing other misdemeanors? More to the point, when was I going to be free of this grueling daily regimen? Clearly, what I was doing was not preventing many students from repeating their offenses. My system was not helping students take more responsibility for themselves.

Recognizing this fact, I began to look differently at what I was doing and I began to see how it did not square with why I had become a principal. I was making students' behavioral problems very public and, in so doing, reducing my chances of learning what was *causing* problems. At the counter, my curt, accusatory, and sometimes sarcastic treatment of habitual offenders was publicly shaming them. (And I was convincing myself that they were beyond being shamed!) In my role as the self-appointed detective, prosecutor, judge, and jury, I guaranteed that *students' views and rights of review* had no chance. In short, there was precious little respect for students or for just treatment in the system.

As an educator, these procedures worked against everything I stood for even though they helped establish my credibility as a new principal. I now see this as tragic. Many new principals, particularly in middle and high schools, feel the same pressure to establish discipline and control and, in the process, to convince others of their competence. Students are sacrificed in this process. Their feelings, ideas, and personal circumstances—the motives that often lead to disciplinary incidents—are neither recognized nor honored. They are taught that power, not justice, will decide their fate, and they will go about their lives at school and after they leave school, too, feeling wronged. For some who are habitual offenders, their identities as "bad-asses" will be confirmed each time we call them publicly to the office and they will learn to relish this attention. In the end, few of those students I called to the office, *learned to become self-disciplining young adults* from my treatment of them.

I eventually learned that to be a just disciplinarian, I needed to do the opposite of the system I inherited. Although it made *me* less conspicuous as a disciplinarian and took more time, I sought out individual "miscreants" and had conversations with them about their behavior, their feelings, and their motivations. These happened at all times and in all places in the school—often in the down times before and after school and during lunches. My conversations made plenty of space for student talk; I learned to question better so that kids would come to recognize the choices they were making. In following up with students, I talked more frequently to the teachers who had "turned them in" and, in the process, involved them more fully in handling their own disciplinary issues. I still meted out punishment, but I did it privately and, more often than not, kids understood their responsibility for the behaviors that led to it.

Most important, I came to see my role not so much as the disciplinarian but as the behavioral counselor. My goal was not primarily to control the school; it was rather to build a just and positive climate and culture among students and adults. I was not just the principal; I was an educator still.

GORDON DONALDSON IS THE DIRECTOR, MAINE ACADEMY FOR SCHOOL LEADERS.

I Probably Am Crazy

MARY BUTTLER

It took almost a week for me to begin to walk on the ground after I was asked to be the principal of Davidson Middle School in San Rafael, California. I soon realized, however, that I had probably gone too far this time, and my ecstasy shifted to terror. I had to be crazy accepting a job with one of the most complex middle schools in Marin County. Did I have the expertise to do the job? Perhaps a more experienced administrator would have been a better choice. This was my first principalship—what if I fell on my face!

My first year began with the need to hire four teachers in August and within days the need to eliminate six class periods due to a low enrollment and a very serious statewide budget crisis that appeared suddenly during September. I had a teacher to evaluate who had unsatisfactory evaluations in the past and lots of written plans for improvement to write and then monitor. In October, one of the new teachers I hired quit to take a job in a high school program with fourteen students in a class rather than the thirty-three students in each of her classes at Davidson. The nightmare continued. A much-needed parcel tax election failed after hours of work by teachers and me. One elementary school in the district wanted to restructure its program to include grades 6–8. The parents at both schools involved the school board, the media, and many parents in their effort. I had regular thoughts of "How many years do I really have to stay as a principal before I can apply for some sort of district job?" I was not sure I would be able to last many years like this!

Then, without warning, things actually got worse. Each and every one of us dreams of being important. One April morning I picked up the local newspaper and found my picture on the front page of the newspaper—right underneath the full-size, colored picture of a gun taken from one of my students. And during the final days of my first year, when four girls were denied the opportunity to attend the final eighth grade graduation dance, their parents rented a local hotel to host a dance of their own at the same time as the school dance.

I list the above problems for one reason. Each of these situations generated a significant number of phone calls and visits from parents, teachers, and the community. I was responsible for being an instructional leader for my school, but there was no room in my day for instructional leadership. I had to deal with parent calls, meetings of all types, district administrators, school board members, and funding agents for the extensive number of programs.

I was determined to make instructional leadership a priority. To do so meant that I spent many nights and weekends at school doing paperwork. I made parent calls at night if possible. I wanted to be visible on campus and in the classrooms during school hours.

As I write this essay, it is now June. I feel as if I have given up a year of my life to survive my first year as principal. I am exhausted, but I do not regret a minute of it. I am proud of my achievements with curriculum and instruction. I had to sacrifice my personal time to establish and maintain a focus of instructional leadership, but the foundation has been laid. I continue to believe next year will be less work. Curriculum had been neglected the past three years as the task of managing the business of school took every free minute for the former principal. I realize that it is not satisfactory for some to consider giving so much personal time to a school program, especially when it takes away from family, but for me the needs of students are extremely important. I also believe that I need to work alongside teachers to model a student-centered approach. Equal access for all students is critical for any school program and can easily be put aside because there are always vocal parents who want the perfect education for their child at the expense of the entire school. I find it to be most challenging to maintain support programs for students and teachers when the building plant needs continue to grow, and to maintain an educational program of quality for every student at the school when many believe that all children cannot learn.

In a never-ending attempt to self-destruct, I asked teachers to complete an evaluation of my performance during that period. The feedback was definitely worth the risk. There were so many positive comments and a real appreciation for the support I provided to teachers. Parents and students also made me feel valued at the end of my first year. I had no idea the impact I had made on the Davidson school community until the end of my first year.

It was only a short time ago that I wanted to consider applying for any district office job available anywhere. Now I can hardly wait for next year to begin at Davidson. I have many more ideas of how to support students and teachers. I have learned that I can survive almost anything. I want to make a difference, and I probably am crazy.

MARY BUTTLER CONTINUES TO BE PRINCIPAL OF DAVIDSON MIDDLE SCHOOL IN SAN RAFAEL, CALIFORNIA.

Principals Must Go Through the Trash

MARK W. LANGE

The 1992–1993 school year was my first as an elementary school principal. I made this fact obvious the first day of July when I stopped by my office. I had left the keys to the school at my home in Lawrence, 150 miles away. I called the secretary, explained what had happened, and she graciously came over to let me in. I mentioned to her this would be the first of many times she would need to bail me out. That prediction was very true. If I could grant one wish to a first-year principal, it would be to have an experienced, competent, cooperative, and patient secretary.

For fourteen years I was an elementary physical education teacher and assistant high school football and track coach. I came to my first year as principal at Lincoln Elementary excited and enthused about the opportunities; I still am. Many of my memories from this past year involve kids. Some brought me pain, some made me mad, and others brought me laughter.

There was the first grade girl still in my office on Friday at four o'clock because mom had not yet picked her up. Mom eventually showed up, with her new husband. She explained they decided to get married and did not expect it to take so long.

I met with her mom the next week to discuss the girl's difficulties at school. She informed me they were moving out of state. She wondered why the girl was withdrawn, why she was struggling. Maybe it has to do with three schools in six months, I wanted to say, or mom getting divorced, remarried, and moving out of state. Just maybe these events contributed to her daughter's difficulties. I still feel guilty for not saying what should have been said.

There was the day three second grade boys came to my office for a visit. One of these boys I knew by name. I began to ask the questions I always asked. "Who has a problem?" "I do," said the first boy. "I do," said the boy on the end. The boy in the middle looked both ways, looked at me, and remained silent. "Who is the only one who can solve this problem?" "I am," said the first boy. "I am," said the boy on the end. The boy in the middle looked both ways, but again remained silent. I asked the last question. "What are you going to do to solve this problem?" The first boy replied, the boy on the end replied, and the boy in the middle looked both ways and looked at me. After a few moments of silence he asked me, "How do these guys know all the answers?" We laughed.

The year affirmed my belief that to lead is to serve. A principal must be willing to ask: what can I do to help you? That simple question is very difficult for some teachers to answer, and some of the answers are very difficult for principals to hear.

The last month of school a second grade girl told me she had dropped two rings in the trash can. I asked her if she had them a long time, "No, I just got them at Wal Mart." I asked if they cost a lot. "No, but I really like them." She looked at me with her blue eyes through red-rimmed glasses. I began digging through the lunch trash, pancakes, sausage, syrup, hash browns, milk cartons, napkins, and other lunch items, piece by piece. After ten minutes of searching we reached the bottom of the trash can. There, lying in a puddle of chocolate milk were two shiny rings. I reached down, picked up the rings, and gave them to the girl as she smiled and said thank you. This moment reminded me that unless we are willing to do the dirty work, we have no right to lead, or expect people to follow.

One mother had been very difficult during the year. There were several times I sat and listened more than I cared to, but there was no doubt she loved her kids and cared about them. The children improved as the year progressed, and during the last week of the school year, the mother stopped by to shake my hand, thank me, and express her pleasure with Lincoln. I treasure that moment. When I ask myself if it is worth all the time, work, and worry, I remember moments such as this and think YES!

MARK LANGE IS THE PRINCIPAL OF LINCOLN ELEMENTARY SCHOOL IN AUGUSTA, KANSAS.

Getting the House in Order

DEBORAH L. HURD

*T*he telephone rang late Friday evening on May 8. It was Father John saying, "The principal's search committee voted unanimously to hire you as principal of St. John's School." The shock and joy that I experienced lasted until Saturday morning when I woke up and realized that I had chosen to do a task that many thought was a losing battle. St. John's was considered a school "at risk." This was the last effort on the part of the diocese to determine if St. John's should remain open. I realized I was invited to make miracles!

The selection of a new principal was a serious and arduous task. The new principal had to turn the school around within a short period of time and prove to the diocese that the school could be a successful venture both academically and financially. I was honored to be selected for this challenge. After ten years serving as assistant principal in a neighboring parish school, I felt the need for a change. I knew the needs of St. John's and felt compelled to give it a try.

I had the opportunity to meet with the parents of St. John's school before school ended in June. At the meeting, I shared with them my belief that parents, school personnel, and the community at large must be actively involved in the education of the children. Parents especially play a unique role and must be involved in all affairs of the school through a strong parent association. The response of the parents was positive.

The halls looked as dreary as some of the local penal institutions. My first task in July was to paint the halls. Fr. John gave me check for $4,000, which I used to purchase paint supplies. I hired people from my previous school to paint, which they did happily, as a gift to me for my new job. I also was able to have the marble floors stripped, waxed, and buffed. The next task was to create some handbooks for students, parents, and teachers. I did this during the month of July, using models from my former school. In addition, I created a school calendar indicating important dates for school closings, parent meetings, and early dismissals. I was ready for September.

The first week of school was calm and uneventful. Enrollment went to 216, which was twenty-five students more than the previous year. I met with all of the students and went over the handbook with them. I talked about suspensions, rules, and expulsions. Above all I talked about striving for excellence.

I also established an advisory board consisting of university, corporate, and government workers. We had divided the board into three areas: fund development, public relations, and academic development. My focus for the academic team was to help develop the areas of math and science by bringing in professionals to do staff development in these areas. I wanted to develop the technology areas and introduce robotics using Lego Logo Programming. This required finding a computer science teacher who could work part-time on this project. We did accomplish that goal and were able to hire a computer teacher for three full days a week. We also established a partnership between the local public university and St. John's allowing students from the seventh and eighth grades to attend the university for four weeks in the summer for hands-on training in math, science, and computer.

My greatest challenge was with the parents. The first three parent meetings were filled. By winter, there was a turnout of twenty-five to fifty. Some parents felt that I was not sharing with them and was much too secretive with my goals and objectives. They wanted to be included in all of my decisions. So I called a meeting of this group of parents and told them all of the plans that I had in mind. I gave them a game plan and a time line for the work. Although overwhelming, it made them feel part of the team. Actually, I discovered that once I worked out that strategy, my work became less troublesome. I learned how to share the load so I wasn't playing all of the instruments while trying to lead the band.

A strategy that I used for my teachers was to reassign them to new grade levels. Many had been teaching the same grade for years. I wanted everyone to feel and act like a first-year teacher who brings a great deal of enthusiasm and motivation to the students. After observing the teachers in the classroom and how they related to the students, I decided who would be best in other grades. I presented my ideas to the teachers individually and asked each one to think about it overnight and let me know. Out of eight teachers, I was able to change six. They were all quite excited. To put a clincher on the school year, I had everybody move out of their classrooms. Some teachers had accumulated years of materials and clutter. By moving, they would be forced to clean out their closets. The teachers' attitudes toward their work became more positive.

Sitting in my office on this last day of June and reflecting on my experiences from this past year, I realize that, I have accomplished some things:

1. A Home School Association in place and ready to go in September
2. A working advisory board composed of merchants, corporate people, university people, and people from city government
3. A kindergarten class that will open in the fall for the first time
4. A school yard with an enclosed playground for preschoolers through second grade designed and constructed by the Housing Preservation Department of our city government at no cost to the school
5. A grant of $20,000 from private patrons who will guarantee funding for at least three years to do any project that will increase enrollment
6. The establishment of the position of assistant principal
7. The establishment of the breakfast program and after school program
8. Departmentalized junior high school grades 6–8

Much of the first year had to do with reorganizing space and with setting the tone for the student body, school personnel, parents, and the community at large. Next year, I will focus more on curriculum with the help of the assistant principal, concentrating on math and science and providing some staff development training in these areas. In addition, I hope to be able to offer adult job-training programs by providing space to a community-based organization.

Deborah L. Hurd is principal of St. Gregory the Great School in New York City.

Trouble and Triumph: A First-Year Experience

NANCY J. MOONEY

My first year as an elementary school principal was both trouble and triumph. First, there was the thrill of being chosen for the principalship from among a tough crowd of competitors. Having spent a teaching career in special education and diagnostic testing, I was a long shot for the job. No one from the special education staff had ever been given the nod, and I was thrilled beyond belief to be the first. Reality set in quickly. Now that I had the job, I was faced with leading a large inner-city school with the highest minority ratio in the city and some of the poorest families.

With fervor, I planned an opening staff meeting that included all the usual business and some staff development centered on creating a discipline plan for the building. Over the summer I had written a teacher handbook that contained written procedures for most of the normal routines of the school such as lunch-count, attendance, fire drills, and substitute teachers. At the faculty meeting I spent time sharing my expectations and listening to theirs. A building leadership team (BLT) was chosen. They helped plan the inservice for the opening faculty meeting, and we got off to a grand start.

Week One was incredible. On opening day there were more than sixty new enrollments. Parents and students were lined up outside the secretary's office, and a few hours seemed like days before all students were in a classroom. I vowed to have a better system the next year. Then came the district head lice check. The team of nurses who arrived one morning to check for head lice found eighty cases. Children were sent home and parents notified. That's when I found out that people in poverty don't have telephones. This problem of communication plagued the school throughout my tenure, but the first year I had no backup plan for such a crisis.

Also that first week, I encountered the federal government's euphemism called "free lunch." Truly, it is a worthwhile program for children whose parents cannot provide a hot lunch daily, but there is nothing free about the bureaucracy involved in processing a form for every child. I could not possibly handle the forms during the day, so each night I took home a pile of forms (more than three hundred in all) and slowly checked, approved, signed, and recorded each form. Thank goodness for an understanding and helpful husband, or I would probably still be working on that pile.

Quickly the urgency of developing a schoolwide discipline plan became apparent. Racial tensions were high and fights were commonplace. Students brought pocket knives and razor blades to school and threatened to use them on each other. Fighting seemed the only strategy they knew for solving a dispute. Child abuse and sexual abuse cases came to my door. I quickly became acquainted with the Division of Family Services and knew the hotline numbers from memory. I saw some tough cases that first year and often as many as eight to ten on a single day. By Christmas, my parents thought I was going to have a nervous breakdown, and I was tired beyond belief.

The tide turned about March of that first year. After one particularly exhausting day, I met a staff member after school. He gave me some of the first feedback I had heard all year. It amounted to little more than encouragement to "hang in there." I needed to hear it in the worst way, and slowly I began to pull out of the depths to "fight back" with what I knew about instructional leadership and a philosophy of schooling.

Communication became a watchword. Throughout the year I had published a weekly calendar for staff that included highlights of the week's events. The calendar took on other dimensions. "A Matter of Principal" was a weekly column, actually a paragraph, that was my opportunity to talk about the things I thought were important to the school. I used a weekly quotation and centered my comments on basic notions of teamwork, perseverance, respect, humor, and caring. The calendar complimented anyone on the staff whose performance exemplified the expectations I had set out at the beginning of the year and the values I held for professional conduct. Even announcements of personal celebrations like the success of a faculty member's child or spouse, a special honor, award or recognition, or the selection to serve on a district committee were applauded in the calendar.

The faculty began to meet to make decisions with me regarding problems and concerns in the school. At first, the creating of a shared vision was awkward because some faculty were unsure of what role they should and could play in deciding the fate of several hundred children and themselves. The basis for mutual trust and respect was laid that first year, a foundation that grew and flourished all the years I was privileged to work with those fine teachers.

There are many more stories of that first year, some wonderful and some wicked. I learned to cope with pressures I never knew existed in the world, and I learned to love a group of children as valuable and important natural resources. Over my seven-year tenure as principal, the discipline plan changed, the fights decreased, and the weapons disappeared. Communication remained of critical importance as well as shared decision making, teamwork, and the creation of a vision of what a grand school can be. I made a lot of mistakes that first year and I worked harder than I have ever worked before or since, but I wouldn't trade that year of frontline experience for any other. Mistakes and all, I made a difference and that was my goal all along.

NANCY MOONEY IS THE SUPERVISOR OF LANGUAGE ARTS IN THE ST. JOSEPH, MISSOURI, SCHOOL DISTRICT.

A Paradoxical Opportunity

SISTER MARIA JUDE

What lies behind us and what lies before us are tiny matters compared to what lies within us.

—William Morrow

It was a small, all-girl, Catholic parish, inner-city high school, located just minutes from the center of Boston, with a student body composed of many cultures—Haitian, Afro-American, Caucasian, Vietnamese, Cambodian, Hispanic, American Indian, Asian, and Portuguese. It was this ethnic and racial diversity that made the school so special to the administration, the faculty, and the students.

In June 1991, I was asked to become "acting principal" of this parish high school, a school where I had been for five years—two years as full-time classroom teacher and three years as vice-principal. I wasn't totally sure how to act as a principal, but I was willing to give it my all. There was no doubt in my mind and heart that it was a right decision even though I had no idea what was to come.

My roles as principal were as diversified as the school. But in each of them, the goal was to encourage young women to grow and develop spiritually, intellectually, culturally, and emotionally as total and unique individuals.

Little did I know that this was to be my first and final performance as principal of this particular high school. In mid-November of my first year, I was told to inform the faculty, staff, parents, and students that the school would close its doors in June, after sixty-nine years of educating young women. This announcement stirred in me an uncomfortable sense of déjà vu since I had been vice-principal of a school that closed under similar circumstances six years earlier in New York.

What I learned from my New York experience and what I had gained from my experiences and challenges while in Boston only made me realize more deeply that in the middle of every difficulty lies opportunity. My opportunity this year was that even though I could not direct the wind, I could adjust the sails and take the ship as far as we could go in the short time we had. I have come to believe that God has a purpose in mind for everything that happens in our lives, and whether we accept it or understand it, He knows what is best for us. I was not going to allow this announcement to diminish a whole school year even though we were living out a paradox—keeping a school alive while at the same time closing its doors. Every journey, no matter how short, has opportunities.

The year was a singular experience, something not many people are asked to live through. It was a time for giving and being truly called to lead.

Since "all eyes" were on the new and "closing" principal—who she is, what she attends to, or what she appreciates or seems to appreciate—it was important to me to be sure that people knew what I valued and how those values related to the long-established SCHOOL CULTURE. My office was located in a very advantageous place near the main office where most of the traffic was, and it was set up so that it didn't welcome only those who were "in trouble." I tried to make sure that I was always on an "up," that I had a sense of humor despite all the frustrations confronting us, that I could be informal as well as formal, that I was approachable, and that I cared very much for each and every individual.

Because I was involved in academics, sports, and extracurricular activities, it wasn't hard for me to convince others that school should be fun and interesting—like a "family,"a community of caring adults and students working together cooperatively—and that I valued a well-rounded person. I also made time to be a constant presence in the school, to be highly visible by visiting classes, working and visiting in the cafeteria in the morning and at lunchtime, and visiting with faculty and students between classes. It was also important to me to learn each and every student's name and background as best I could.

As I stood at the podium in the sanctuary of the parish church on May 21, just before presenting each member of the Class of 1992 with her diploma and knowing that it was my final curtain call, I shared these thoughts with the entire cast—the faculty and staff, the parents, the students, the Class of 1992, and all our friends:

> I thank each of you for what you have added to the spirit of our school. For without you, respect for and understanding of our many different cultures would have been lacking in every way. It has been a pleasure for me to wake up each morning and know I was going to spend my day with you. I couldn't think of any other place I would have liked to have spent my energies and my days—you are my energizers.
>
> You have a lot of potential, commitment, understanding, and love. You are the future and the future is yours; I depend on you, make a difference. Do not worry or fret about what you leave behind. Take with you the lessons you have learned and the ideals and values that you have added to your individual person. Continue to have faith in yourselves, faith in your abilities, faith in your dreams, and faith in your responsibilities.
>
> The time for moving on is now, creating new relationships,
> new challenges,
> new memories.

One of the questions frequently asked of me throughout the year was "If you had known in July 1991 what you'd be asked to do, would you have taken on the role, responsibility, and challenge of being principal?" My answer was always a very humble and unequivocal *"YES."*

SISTER MARIA JUDE IS VICE-PRINCIPAL FOR ACADEMIC AFFAIRS AT BISHOP FEEHAN HIGH SCHOOL IN ATTLEBORO, MASSACHUSETTS.

The Tip of the Iceberg

DAVID H. WRIGHT

*E*veryone knows that the largest part of an iceberg is below the surface of the water. Well, life's experiences can be like that too. What is visible may seem very manageable and not very intimidating. Looming below the surface, however, is an enormous amount of mass that will not easily give in to any kind of force. This is how I found the principalship.

Finally, it happened! That phone call that puts a knot in your stomach and causes your once-confident voice to shake and sound very much like an adolescent with overactive hormones. I was being offered a position as elementary principal. At that moment I was feeling every emotion that can be described. The master plan was working! I was going to accept. Iceberg sighted!

At the first opportunity, I gathered the family around the map, and while pointing to the town I shared the news. The children ran crying to their rooms, and my wife cried all over the map. The iceberg was getting bigger.

The day finally arrived when I officially reported to school. The elementary handbook had been approved and sent off to the printers; the secretary was busy preparing attendance records and class lists, taking inventory of new materials, assembling first-day packets for teachers and students, and completing a million other tasks that are traditionally done at the beginning of the school year. I was busy being briefed by the superintendent about procedures, board policy, supervision of the special education and Chapter 1 programs and the day-to-day operations of the school. After the first week I was completely exhausted, which really scared me because the staff and students wouldn't be in school for another three weeks. The full extent of the iceberg's mass was strongly suspected.

That first week of school finally arrived, and as with any new marriage everyone was nervous, very forgiving, tolerant, and understanding. Knowing that all situations don't last forever, I still wanted this wonderful rapport to last the entire school year. Who was I kidding! What I didn't realize was that from the very beginning I was considered by the older staff members (with a zillion years of experience in the very same building) as a "nice boy" who meant well. I was a "nice boy" until I started suggesting some subtle changes in the day-to-day routine, and I then became the bad boy on the block. The iceberg's depth below the surface was at fifteen fathoms.

"Didn't you know you were interfering with tradition?" "The teachers have never done it that way before!" "That's not the way we do things around here!" These battle cries rang through the building *and the universe*. It was October and the honeymoon was over. The *entire* mass of the iceberg above and below the surface was finally realized.

Now was the time for some reflective thought and analysis. I operated on the premise of "we is smarter than me." I had scheduled regular staff meetings for the purpose of information sharing, group problem solving, and decision-making sessions. After trying hard to keep staff members involved, still there were complaints and dissatisfaction, and I was frustrated.

When situations get too overwhelming with "principal stuff," my secretary can find me with the kindergarten students laughing, playing, and just plain getting excited about being in school. I get more pleasure going into the kindergarten room to learn how to color all over again with such wise and learned six-year-olds than anywhere else in the building. I enjoy visits by the students to the office to work on class assignments, talk about the school day, or just discuss a favorite project. Whenever the frustrations get too great, I return to the children and the teaching to remind myself what this business is all about.

I survived the first year with only a dent in the rudder and minor damage to the bridge.

DAVID WRIGHT IS THE ELEMENTARY PRINCIPAL OF THE ALBION PUBLIC SCHOOLS IN ALBION, NEBRASKA.

Up the Hawsepipe

THOMAS EISMEIER

There is an expression in the Merchant Marine that describes officers who are former deckhands or engine room wipers and rose to licensed rank not by going to college—not by graduating from one of the seven maritime academies—but by passing examinations after learning on the job. Such people are said to come up the hawsepipe.

—John McPhee, *Looking for a Ship*

After about fifteen years teaching underprivileged kids in Chicago, overprivileged kids in Brooklyn, and plain country kids in Vermont, I came "up the pipe" to become the teaching principal at a small, rural elementary school. I had begun my teaching career with little more preparation than the proverbial good intentions. By the time I became interested in administration, I had a realistic idea of how schools worked—or didn't work—and an idealistic determination to improve them.

Teaching principals in Vermont are not required to hold an administrative license, but having come up the anchor chain, I decided to take the courses to earn a license. My performance on the job, moreover, proved to be a series of personal quizzes, tests, exams, and institutional trials that lent depth and meaning to the professional title of principal.

New principals seem to have a natural tendency to try to please everybody and do everything. When aided and abetted by parents, teachers, and school board members, this tendency can become harmful to a principal's health. As the school's first "real" administrator, I think I suffered more than most from the I'll-do-it-myself syndrome.

I realized early on that I had to set strict guidelines about my availability as a principal. I sent a letter home asking parents to call me either before 7:30 or after 11:30 A.M., when my classroom responsibilities ended; otherwise they could leave a message with the secretary. I made it clear to teaching staff that I did not want to be interrupted in the classroom for anything less than a natural disaster. In the meantime, word spread swiftly that a new and highly paid person was available at the school to listen to complaints, sympathize with real or imagined grievances, and tend to chores that nobody else wanted to do. Parents appeared at my classroom door demanding immediate satisfaction to their problems. Kids from other classes streamed into my room bearing notes that read either that they had been bad or that a toilet was clogged. There wasn't much to do except put out the fires as they flared up and hope that the small crises would subside. Eventually, people realized that I was not on call twenty-four hours a day, and the teaching part of my schedule settled into a pleasant and productive routine.

I was just as strict about maintaining my administrative role as I was about preserving the integrity of my daily teaching time. Outside the classroom I metamorphosed into the principal. The fifth/sixth graders in my classroom were surprisingly adaptive to this shift in roles when I visited them with their "other" teacher in the afternoons. Some of the younger students, whose classes I visited every day, were shocked to hear from older siblings that the principal—the man in the tie—was also a teacher.

Leaving the classroom responsibilities behind for the day, I was ready for the morning's accumulation of mail, notes, phone calls, and kids and adults waiting to see me. I dealt with the demands as best I could, sometimes comparing the whole operation to a triage in a M*A*S*H unit. Somehow, though, at the end of the day, no matter how long I stayed, not everything was completed. I lugged home a briefcase weighted both with kids' assignments and with administrative forms and letters. I worked evenings; I worked weekends. I even hired a substitute for myself so that I could spend at least one full day observing and recording the school's established rhythms and routines inside and out.

While responding to people's immediate needs I also invested considerable time and effort in organizing schedules, systems, and procedures to make the school less dependent on me personally. For example, because we were in mild crisis when I first arrived, I practically force-fed a Glasser-based discipline model to the staff and parents. We used staff meeting and inservice time to discuss kids' behavior and how to respond without reflexively sending them to the office to be scolded by the principal. I knew we were making progress when parents began asking for more information so that they could try using time-out and planning techniques at home.

My first year at West Fairlee was rich, varied, challenging, and difficult. The job description for the administrative half of my position included:

- Lighting the pilot on the hot water heater when the janitor wasn't around— and wondering why I always seemed to be wearing light-colored clothes on these occasions
- Directing a backhoe late at night after part of the septic system failed and no one could remember exactly where it was buried
- Calling substitutes at 6:00 A.M. and repeating to myself that teachers and staff members didn't get sick on purpose
- Developing budgets and then cutting them
- Supervising and evaluating the staff while trying not to run afoul of union rules
- Meeting the superintendent periodically for a reality check
- Putting the tether ball back up when the rope broke
- Officiating kids' soccer games
- Participating on the district's administrative team with all the clout of a small third world country on the UN Security Council
- Reminding angry kids not to yell or use four-letter words
- Reminding angry parents not to yell or use four-letter words
- Reminding myself that I might be making a difference

Looking back at that first year now that I am a full-time principal in another, larger school, I did not realize how difficult it was until I stopped doing it.

THOMAS EISMEIER IS THE PRINCIPAL AT MORETOWN ELEMENTARY SCHOOL IN MORETOWN, VERMONT.

The Lessons Learned

IRA E. BOGOTCH

*I*f I had known then, what I know now . . . ah, there's the rub. Today, as a professor of educational leadership at the University of New Orleans, I study and write about beginning principals. But, of course, what I do today didn't matter when I first started being a principal. What mattered then was that I had a job to do, an overwhelming job, for which few are ever ready when they begin.

Thoughts about my first faculty meeting, my first parent-teacher night, my first accreditation report . . . everything was my first! . . . all merge together. I remember how faculty meetings changed from being primarily social and business meetings to becoming real professional development conferences led by teachers; how teachers learned to communicate with parents about what teachers did in class and how that related to the overall purposes of the school curriculum; and how the school's earning of accreditation turned on outrageous luck.

In 1988–89, I assumed the principalship of a private, sectarian elementary school that had a long-standing reputation for the caring and nurturing of children but was also known for its weak academics. The goal, impressed upon me by the school's board, was to improve curriculum and instruction without disrupting the positive climate for teachers and students. It was obvious that the teachers enjoyed teaching at this school and that they believed in their students' potential for academic achievement. Their job satisfaction, however, did not translate into effective teaching. Although most of the teachers expressed some degree of criticism of the school's textbooks, the curriculum-in-use was the textbooks themselves coupled with teacher's editions and commercial, supplementary materials. Too many of the daily classroom activities were limited to the chronology of textbooks and the suggestions of the editors.

Here were talented teachers who were not using their talents effectively, and who, despite their congeniality did not work together as cohesive and collegial faculty in planning and implementing a balanced or articulated curriculum. On these issues, their message to me was quite clear: unless I was going to make curricular decisions the textbooks would have to suffice. They were not going to make such decisions.

Thus, I began a process aimed at changing attitudes, building teacher self-confidence, rediscovering or learning skills, and implementing a better academic program. The process was essentially inductive: we (1) held weekly lunchtime staff meetings to discuss the findings from effective school and effective teaching literatures, (2) informally visited each other's classrooms, (3) promoted and shared new ideas seen in and out of the classrooms, (4) scheduled one formal classroom observation based on teaching behaviors associated with effectiveness (e.g., time on task, monitoring student performance, and classroom management), and (5) collaborated in designing self-evaluation projects based on classroom observations that were shared with the rest of the staff.

While this emphasis on academics resulted in some notable changes during that first year, the overall goal of identifying the principles upon which to build the curriculum was not attained. Teachers were still teaching material independent of what others had done previously and with no real idea of how student knowledge progresses through grade school. Progress within any one classroom did not influence changes throughout the school. Moreover, without any unifying principles as a school curriculum framework, some of the positive steps taken during year one to advance the academic program did not see the light of day in year two.

Somewhat frustrated by the lack of teacher self-directedness, I wrote a grade-by-grade sequence based on some general learning principles upon which we could all agree, such as self-esteem, technical student proficiency, global literacy, tolerance, and self-awareness. The sequenced topics were not a curriculum, but rather consensual views within which to explore grade-level metaphors— school as family theatre, being successful by apprenticing, discovering and caring for what's around us, taking a cross-country trip, and going around the world in 180 school days.

Despite the groundwork laid in consensus building and collegiality, the changes suggested by the ambiguous metaphorical themes created, for a while, a decline in faculty morale. Most of the teachers urged me privately to clarify the meaning of these metaphors as they related to specific grade-level curriculum and teaching assignments. I had hoped that over time and without my direction, some of the teachers would start to move away from their textbook-driven curriculum, and their teaching would become more child-focused, skill-oriented, and creative.

Some teachers began to explore materials and give substance and meaning to the sequenced metaphors—all for the next school year. Another sign that attitudes were changing was that as a faculty we were able to implement other new and significant programmatic improvements without a great deal of turmoil. For example, new grading standards were clarified, and a more rigorous standardized test was adopted that reflected greater confidence in ourselves.

As a first-year principal, I also had the experience of going through an accreditation visit. Amidst the extra pressure of this close scrutiny, the leader of the visiting team asked us to hold a fire drill. The bells rang and the children dutifully exited the building, moving quickly to their assigned places across the street. One of my responsibilities as principal was to check the student bathrooms before I left to make sure every child was safely outside. In my eagerness to join the students and teachers, I almost decided to skip that step, but at the last moment I changed my mind. And lucky for me I did. The boys' room was empty, but standing in one of the girls' room stalls like an inspector general was the leader of the accreditation team waiting to see how thorough I was. He smiled, and the two of us walked out of the building together.

What lessons can be learned from these experiences? Clearly, the private school context permitted me and the faculty far greater choice about the content of curriculum. Yet, the dynamic social processes are essentially the same for teachers within all schools.

LESSON ONE

If I were to begin anew, I would start with the program adopted during year two, that is, working with teachers to define the school's philosophy of education and to develop a schoolwide consensus on the principles of learning. To improve schools, teachers and administrators as well as parents need to have answers to the why's of their behaviors if improvement is going to occur. Philosophy precedes curricular development and instructional methods, not vice versa.

LESSON TWO

Restructuring an ongoing school program takes more time than creating new programs. The institution's history regarding the way things have been done previously is important for restructuring. Leadership needs to emphasize academics and to create an environment that supports change. There are certainly quicker paths to change, but restructuring is more than a one- or even two-year effort. Even when the innovation is considered successful, it does not insure its institutional continuation.

LESSON THREE

No instructional leader has unilateral power. Such leadership is a matter of mutual dependency. Teachers' commitment and effort appear to count most in determining continued progress of a newly created program. Leadership can try to create meaningful incentives in terms of people's career choices. But the willingness to act over time rests with teachers.

LESSON FOUR

The demands and realities of our jobs as teachers and school administrators are not structured to permit sufficient reflection or time to adjust to the dynamics of change. Good teachers and administrators are overworked. School leaders need to make time for teachers and themselves by first taking away some of the present responsibilities before adding new work.

LESSON FIVE

Our jobs in education are never finished or fully realized. Restructuring requires sustained direction and commitment, regardless of personnel changes.

LESSON SIX

Hope for your share of outrageous good luck.

As a professor, I am now helping others to engage in the never-ending work of educating others. I keep rewriting the script I follow in my classes, constantly seeking to improve. The only script I can't rewrite or correct is the one I lived as a beginning principal.

IRA E. BOGOTCH IS ASSISTANT PROFESSOR IN EDUCATIONAL LEADERSHIP AT THE UNIVERSITY OF NEW ORLEANS.

The Year of Living Dangerously

THOMAS A. DRAZDOWSKI

As we entered the music classroom, there was Jimmy standing on a chair, swinging his arms in rhythm to gain momentum for his flight, all the while looking menacingly down at the teacher. Below him was a row of four guitars, all neatly arranged at equal distances and soon to be victims of a lethal game of guitar hop frog. Sister Dominica calmly but firmly directed Jimmy to come down safely from his perch, deflecting his vulgarities with a matter-of-factness that de-escalated the situation and my own strong urge to pummel the offender for saying such nasty things to a nun. As the anger started to dissipate from Jimmy's body, he slowly stood erect, glanced one more time at the teacher, then jumped from the chair, skillfully missing the first guitar. He headed out the door and toward my office. As I silently followed behind, I began to wonder what I had gotten myself into. It was only the first twenty minutes of my first day in my first job as a principal, and already I had found that there was much my professors forgot to teach me in graduate school. My true education had just begun.

The setting for my first year as principal was a small private secondary school that had been established by an order of nuns to serve children who had been labeled socially and emotionally disturbed. The students came to the school from around the state, mostly referred to us by their former school districts, child welfare agencies, or the juvenile courts. Out of one hundred plus students, approximately sixty females were residents of the school as well, giving them a chance to escape from some bad home environments while allowing them to concentrate on school studies and to receive professional counseling. The teachers, all certified in their content areas as well as special education, were assigned from the local state intermediate unit. Having been hired by the good sisters, I was expected to walk the delicate balance between the private and the public sector and help develop a school that was consistent with the total-treatment milieu. Despite Jimmy, or maybe because of him, I knew that first day I would like this place. Much more than "traditional" education was going on here. Whole lives were being transformed. Shortly my own would be added to the list.

As I reviewed the long inventory of duties on my job description, many seemed to fit with my expectations for the role of principal, such as providing leadership in improving classroom instruction and professional development of staff, designing and improving the curriculum, preparing the school budget, and maintaining communications with the state board of private academic schools. Because this was a small school and virtually a one-person office, the list also included making the schedule of classes, providing academic and career counseling, maintaining an effective system of student record-keeping and the effective execution of administrative details, such as receiving supplies, doing inventories, answering correspondence, distributing school mail, and assigning lockers. The list covered three pages with thirty such items. I would need a very big closet to store all the hats I was expected to wear. Most principals do.

The items that would consume most of my school day, however, appeared at the end of the list: maintain satisfactory principal-student informal relationships, order, and discipline. Sister Dominica had the title of "crisis intervention specialist" and would assist me in this area. All teachers had access to a telephone, and when a lid was about to blow, my office would get a call. These kids needed lots of extra TLC, and finding the balance between hug and hardnose was a continual challenge for me. But Sister was a wonderful teacher, and the experienced staff were willing to share their collective expertise.

As with any school, I quickly found that the teachers were its strength and soul. Each performed heroic efforts each day, tempering all actions with care and compassion. The ways of the good sisters seemed to rub off on whomever they came in contact with. There was Ted, the science teacher, whose garden and greenhouse cultivated so much more than just fresh produce for the school kitchen. Jill, the math teacher, whose dry humor and unflappable nature gave kids a sense of security in facing both the subject matter and the perils of life. Greg, the beloved art teacher, whose classes gave the kids a creative outlet for a host of pent-up emotions. Each member of the twelve-person faculty brought special talents to bear, sharing not only knowledge but humanness, helping to make the journey a reward in itself.

And of course, there were the kids. Jimmy, the guitar lover, who had a hair-trigger temper and had already blown through several schools and foster homes. Gloria, who after losing her mother in a fire, survived on the streets of a major city by living with "cousins" until a child welfare agency finally tracked her down. Margaret, who slept each night cuddling a baseball bat, used in her dreams to protect her from a frightening past. Many of the kids had suffered physical and/or sexual abuse and needed a safe environment in order to have a chance. Several had been arrested for prostitution, others for involvement with drugs. Mark had taken part in an armed robbery. Jake had accidentally shot and killed his brother while playing with a gun. A nation at risk indeed. Our students were a collection of derailed lives looking for guidance and direction, all brought together by fate and circumstance to this very special school.

That first year of twelve-hour days passed quickly. There were setbacks and failures but also many of the so-called "small victories" that continue to compel us forward. As a principal, as faculty, and as students, we faced each day and grew and learned together. Six of our twelve graduating seniors that year were accepted into post-secondary schools. All returned to the mainstream of life to continue the daily struggle but with a newfound confidence and perspective on life that only a loving environment can provide.

My educational career continues to take many turns, from teaching in the Alaskan bush (yes, the show *Northern Exposure* was my life!) to getting my doctorate and becoming a teacher of teachers. Challenges all, but challenges met with the wisdom gained from that first year as a principal. I've had a new compass to guide my life. As Frost so aptly pointed out, the road less traveled by has made all the difference. For anyone approaching that first year as principal, my advice is to look forward to this opportunity to be transformed.

THOMAS A. DRAZDOWSKI IS A FACULTY MEMBER IN THE EDUCATION DEPARTMENT AT KING'S COLLEGE.

Tale of the First Year

MARY ANN SINKKONEN

*W*ho, me? A principal? That was a recurring thought that first year. A confessor, confidante, facilitator, humorist, director, teacher, parent, and friend. That's who I was. Prepared or not, I had the job.

The pace of a principalship is fast. A principal makes split-second decisions, and with practice over time, hopes they are thoughtful. The following description is aimed toward moving the reader into the environment of the principalship. Feel what it's like and wonder, would you want the job?

A snapshot of a day:

7:30 A.M. I find that during the night someone squirted glue into all the exterior door locks. The custodian, who arrived at 7:00 A.M. has called the maintenance department. The doors have been deglued but I check them to be sure. All are OK.

7:50 A.M. A phone call from the sub desk. The secretary will be absent and there is no sub for the day. I close the school library and reassign the clerk to the office. She had subbed in that capacity before. This makes sense to me but not to the head librarian.

8:00 A.M. A parent walks into the office and announces that he would like to speak to the principal. I respond. There is a problem. As a high school and collegiate basketball player, he is concerned because all of our hoops are netless. How can a decent game of "B" ball be played with a netless hoop? I listen and share with him the reality of outdoor courts and community use during non-school hours. I recount the almost perpetual replacement of nets that occurs when nets are installed on outdoor hoops. Practicality is not an acceptable reason for him, and he assures me the matter will be taken up with someone at the district level.

8:25 A.M. A teacher reminds me to come by the classroom at 9:15 to enjoy the fifth grade performance of their Civil War play.

8:27 A.M. Art docent arrives and notices that the portfolio for her presentation today (five classrooms) has not arrived from the previous week's school. I make phone calls to see if we can locate the material. Her first appointment is at 8:45 A.M.

8:35 A.M. I am on my way to pick up the portfolio at another school.

8:30 A.M. While I am on the road, the school bell rings to start the day.

8:50 A.M. The portfolio is in the hands of the docent and she walks to the first class of the day, just five minutes late. The head librarian is waiting for me. The issue is reassigning the library clerk to the office without asking the head librarian. I describe my responsibility and let it be known that in the best interest of the school, I would do it again. Case disagreeably closed.

9:00 A.M. The custodian walks in. "There is a guy practicing his golf swing on the back field." I suggest that he ask the fellow to leave since the grounds are closed during school hours. "The guy has a Doberman with him and I'm not getting near the dog." I look around and not seeing any other person to approach the golfer, I walk out to the field. The golfer is cooperative. The dog is quiet and obedient. The field is cleared of golfer and dog.

9:15 A.M. The fifth grade play. What a joy! The students have written the script from the point of view of eyewitnesses. Their dialogue takes the form of letters to various persons. Their grasp of key ideas, emotions, politics, geography, etc., is impressive. Parents in attendance are awed by the depth of understanding.

10:05 A.M. On my way back to the office, I meet four sixth grade students who are putting up the ancestor chart on the window of the multiuse room. We have been studying heritage as a theme across the school. This class has volunteered to collate all of the information and to chart the ancestry of all of our students.

10:15 A.M. A third grade classroom for a formal teacher observation. Solve the problem: "With the materials provided, build a shelter for a family lost in the forest." There are criteria, parameters outlined in the instructions to the groups. At the planning conference, the teacher has asked that I note the clarity of his directions with regard to the nature of any student questions about the task. He also would like feedback about the students' on-task behavior.

11:15 A.M.   Back in the office, I begin to reflect on the teacher observation. A parent has called to express concern about my decision to continue past practice regarding "no dances" for sixth graders. I return the call.

11:45 A.M.   A half hour later I return to the observation but am diverted by a yard supervisor. "There is no water running in the drinking fountains or faucets." I ask the secretary to call the water district and see what's happening. We are about to dismiss 570 students for lunch. We are told that due to construction a few blocks away, all water has been turned off for the next half hour. I decide that we need to alert all students that restrooms, fountains, and sinks are off limits until 12:15. Only emergencies should come to the office restroom. The yard supervisors and I lock student restrooms.

12:15 P.M.   Water is turned on again. There is the anticipated rush to the restrooms. I'm helping with traffic to the restrooms and drinking fountains.

1:00 P.M. The after-lunch roundup, cleanup and investigation. This is the daily routine, the after-lunch recess report from the yard supervisors. Today, only one incident. A fourth grader was roughed up by a sixth grader because the fourth grader had pushed his way onto the sixth grade basketball court and would not take "no" for an answer when told to go to the fourth grade court.

1:15 P.M.   I try to eat lunch. As I open the brown bag, I hear our secretary say, "I think you better talk with our principal." When I hear those words I know that she has tried everything and this could take a while. The person I see is a parent who is concerned with the school dress code. "Why can't the girls wear shorts to school?" This discussion is just the beginning of what materializes into a major parent/student conflict over a period of several months and culminates in a survey and a change in the "Shorts Rule."

1:30 P.M.   I'm back to the lunch bag, when I realize it is time for me to go to a classroom where I have been invited to see weekly art centers. Close the lunch bag.

2:00 P.M.   The early arrival students, (we have an early/late schedule for grades 1–3) are dismissed. We are short one bus supervisor so I stand bus duty for twenty minutes.

2:20 P.M.   I notice I am hungry and that I haven't been to the restroom since I left home at 7:00 A.M. I head for the restroom but I am distracted by the sounds of the fifth grade chorus in the multiuse room. This session is sometimes difficult for the music teacher, and I decide to stop in. The little cherubs, those fifth graders, need a few glances from me to focus on "Oh What a Beautiful Morning."

2:25 P.M.   Yes, the restroom is on my way back to the office.

2:30 P.M.   While I was on campus, four phone messages came in. I note that one of them is from the superintendent. I make that call and learn that our school has been selected for a visit from our local state congressman next week. We discuss the details, and I begin to consider a schedule.

2:45 P.M.   The lunch bag is looking tired. I'm thinking that tomorrow's lunch will be better. I'm not really hungry anyway.

3:00 P.M.   Dismissal. Again, I'm on bus duty.

3:15 P.M.   I begin to read the day's mail. I jot down appointments for meetings. I attend to paperwork related to the earlier teacher observation.

3:30 P.M.   Teachers begin to drop in. The most frequently used phrase is "Got a minute?" The conversations center around: What about this or that field trip? What about this or that student? What about this or that parent? What about this or that teaching strategy?

4:30 P.M.   Back to paperwork: observation, budgets, weekly community newsletter, staff bulletin, notes to teachers, thank-you letters, express mail to district personnel.

6:00 P.M.   Walk to the parking lot. One day of this school year has passed.

Why would anyone do this job? Are we all crazy? For me the job was the hardest job I have ever had and the most rewarding. The school community is like a big classroom. I loved classroom teaching, and I loved the principalship. After fifteen years of classroom teaching, then three years in staff development, the principalship was a logical step for me.

Looking back on that first year, here's what helped me most:

· keeping a journal so I could write, reread, and reflect
· listening, being a sounding board so people could discover that the solutions were within themselves
· having a friend with whom I could role play and who could help me better prepare to face awkward situations
· asking questions

- tending to the obvious like repainting the staff room, repairing broken window blinds, replacing chalkboards
- talking socially with the staff in the lunchroom
- recognizing and celebrating successes

If there was anything routine it was being everywhere: in classrooms, out on the yard, in the library, the computer lab, in the special education classrooms.

The best advice I received as I was beginning that first year was, "Use your position to say, 'Yes'."

MARY ANN SINKKONEN IS THE COORDINATOR OF CATEGORICAL PROGRAMS FOR THE NOVATO UNIFIED SCHOOL DISTRICT IN CALIFORNIA.

Wings: My First Year as a Principal

ELAINE M. PACE

*T*he anticipated phone call echoed in my ears, "Congratulations, Elaine! We'd like to offer you the position of elementary school principal in Parsippany." "Yes!" I shouted inwardly, while outwardly I replied quite professionally, "Why, thank you. I'm thrilled. I have a few questions, but I'd be delighted to accept."

Acceptance. Another challenge. Reach for the stars, I had always believed, and you'll fly far higher than if you reach for something on a level with yourself. I reached.

I always liked Disraeli's words, "We are not creatures of circumstance; we are creators of circumstance." Here was my opportunity to be a creator. Truthfully it was "community" I wanted to create. I had been a director of staff development previously, working out of the central office. While I had had an opportunity to touch lives indirectly by designing programs and training teachers, I remained Queen for a Day in that former job. I yearned for the opportunity to become more a part of what I created.

Not until later when I read Roland Barth's wonderful book, *Improving Schools from Within,* did I begin to grapple with the meaning of "the school as community." I learned at the Harvard Principals' Center just how affective the principal's job was. I had led communities of children, but a community of adults presented a different challenge. My acquaintance with the work of Drs. Judith Arin-Krupp and Sarah Levine was invaluable in helping me understand the stages of adult development and the concept of the

50

adult learner. The 1990 U.S. Department of Education monograph, *The Principal's Role in Shaping School Culture,* defined my new role succinctly. I would shape school culture as a symbol . . . a potter . . . a poet . . . an actor . . . and a healer. It was as simple as that! All jest aside, that monograph was a treasure. Then, once I learned to create the culture, I would need to learn the valuable skill of how to "reframe" it according to Drs. Lee Bolman and Terry Deal. But I'm getting ahead of myself. Back to the first year of principalship.

"Well begun is half done," Aristotle proclaimed. I made a good beginning. The "agreeables" joined my camp right away; the "wait and sees" within a year. With the help of a perceptive and faithful secretary and a small cadre of reassuring staff members, I managed to maintain relatively open communication with the "skeptics."

The P.T.A. was another matter. An overly zealous group of novice parents met my initial efforts with consternation. Accustomed to unchecked power in the wake of a former absentee principal, this small but vocal group of parent leaders challenged my every effort to steer the starship Littleton back onto course. When I increased security so that strangers would no longer be able to enter the school at all hours, I was accused of not welcoming parents. When I formed a collaborative advisory council of parents, teachers, and school leaders, I was accused of trying to subvert the power of the P.T.A. This problem required a long-range view. Veteran principal colleagues convinced me that I should rise above the fray, remain open and collaborative, and gradually nurture my own followers. That took nearly two years, but the rewards were worth every step in the struggle and every iota of self-discipline required of me. In my third year as principal, I bravely hired the president of the P.T.A. as one of my staff members.

When I was a staff developer, I remember learning about attribution theory. Attribution theory says that some things happen purely out of luck, some out of innate ability, some out of task difficulty, and some out of effort. That memory culled from my repertoire helped me grapple with the predictably unpredictable in my first year of principalship. Principals are generally people who enjoy control. Attribution theory helped me to understand what I could and could not control, a valuable lesson in that first year. Most of us become principals because we are willing to expend the effort to control well. The challenge is how to share that control with our staff, our colleagues, and our community. I learned to beware first impressions. One colleague whom I had thought would be my best friend turned out to be relentlessly competitive. I was determined in easing myself out of that yoke. A teacher's camaraderie, in another case, proved to be self-serving and not committed to fostering a wholesome, trusting culture in our building. We should invite others into our "inner circle" judiciously. We want our friends, not our foes, in there with us. Sharing control is paramount for a good principal, but sharing is an art not developed fully in the first year of principalship. It is the reward, in the long term, for a job well done. It makes the job a lot less lonely, too!

There are surely certain events that unexpectedly engineer hours, sometimes days and weeks, of our time, forcing the postponement of even our most routine tasks. I think of my first six weeks as principal and of the bus driver who wrapped one of our school buses around a tree en route home one afternoon. The driver, sufficiently relaxed from the alcohol in his body, escaped unharmed. That accident occurred less than five minutes after our last elementary school child had alighted from the bus.

Attribution theory also says that outcomes are often determined by innate ability that surely directs the progress we may or may not make as principals. I dealt with a middle-class, suburban neighborhood where many parents took pride in an elitism of holding P.T.A. offices, sponsoring their own school board candidate, running soccer and Little League, Girl Scouts, Boy Scouts, Cubs, Daisies, and enough fund-raisers to contribute approximately $15,000 per year to our school. The innate ability was surely here. This culture may sound ideal, but, despite its assets, it makes the school a hard place for a principal to be a hero. What could I do to make a real difference in this place?

Task difficulty is the third component of attribution theory. How difficult is this task of being a principal? On many days it seems insurmountable, even in the best of schools. Because we have chosen, as one scholar says, "to take abuse for a living," there's only one way to deal with the difficulty of our task—simplify, simplify, simplify. We can only deal effectively with one or two issues at a time. Prioritizing was very important for me. Having already tried to be a super mom, a super teacher, a super wife, a super principal, and a super person, I realize that I can't do it all and still be super! I've become better at delegating and focusing all my energies on only one to two things at a time. Then I turn my back and go home. The work never fails to greet me the next morning.

Finally comes effort. Effort we can control. I'd venture to guess that most principals comprise a premium group of overachievers. After all, most of us became principals because we were successful teachers. If we weren't such overachievers, we'd still be teaching—a profession most of us loved!

When I was a college senior, I devoured the poetry of T.S. Eliot. One of my favorite quotes continues to live with me as I venture on the journey of principalship. In "Little Gidding," the fourth of Eliot's *Four Quartets,* he writes:

> We shall not cease from exploration.
> And the end of all our exploring
> Will be to arrive where we started
> And know the place for the first time.

The hope of our exploring is that as principals we discover how to shape the cultures of our schools knowingly, with compassion, and, most important, with wisdom!

ELAINE PACE IS THE PRINCIPAL OF THE LITTLETON SCHOOL IN PARSIPPANY, NEW JERSEY.

Lives of a Rural Principal

EDWARD ROBERT WILKENS

In the days before public kindergarten became popular, Mrs. Smithson's private, half-day preschool prepared me reasonably well for life as an elementary school student. I entered first grade in 1959, moderately socialized and equipped with reading and math readiness.

Two years ago, after nineteen years as a student, I reentered elementary school. This time as a principal. And this time, despite an array of academic credentials garnered since 1959, I was probably no better prepared than Mrs. Smithson had made me for first grade.

I did have a B.A. in English literature and an M.Ed. focused on administration and planning, with courses such as Public School Finance 344, School Law 312, Curriculum Concepts and Development 377, and Organizational Leadership 308 behind me. The courses were interesting and necessary. Actually, only some of the courses were interesting—but, according to the state certification board, all were necessary.

Surely no people on the state certification board were thinking about a rural elementary school when they determined the standards. If they had, they would have included three areas that can be broadly catalogued as Mechanics, Nature, and People.

During my first two years as principal of a small, rural elementary school I encountered a spectrum of situations, problems, and emergencies, none of which was even peripherally considered during my graduate training for this job. That is no one's fault; it is simply not possible to anticipate, much less gain practice necessary to cope with, such aspects of the principalship as backed-up sewer lines, lost teeth, a wandering bull, a parent with a clumsy left hook, and the People's Republic of China.

ENCOUNTER WITH A BUS

Of mechanics, nature, and people, the area that I am least comfortable with and knowledgeable about is mechanics. Yet, one snowy, windy morning a bus driver thought it essential that I join him in inspecting the cracked leaf springs on a bus. We went to the lot, and he slid under the bus. I was content to crouch gingerly alongside and peer under the vehicle, avoiding the oiled and muddied slush as much as possible. Not satisfied with such a cursory investigation, the driver urged me under the bus with him. He wanted me to be as informed as he, so I ignored the fact that I was wearing my best suit for a meeting later that day at the state department, and I crawled—as much as possible on toes and fingertips—under the bus to the damage site to frown and shake my head knowingly at the cracked springs.

Since that morning I have grown even more familiar with our buses. I have delivered gas, transported damaged heater coils, ridden in, helped jump-start, and driven the buses enough to satisfy any latent curiosity I may have had about their mechanical psyches.

STEMMING THE TIDE

If I am not an accomplished mechanic, I am even less a plumber, but I have gained the sensitivity no longer to question why plumbers get $25 per hour. At the end of an otherwise uneventful day, I met with a substitute teacher to ask about her experience with the class, thank her, and say good night. Just before leaving, she turned and said, "Oh, by the way, you should probably check the class bathroom. We had a few problems this morning."

She left, and I checked. The morning's "few problems" had grown to a tide of sewage. Second graders are not ecologically minded, as evidenced by their wanton use of toilet paper. Fortunately, there is an inch-high threshold leading to the bathroom, and the water had not yet crested that dike. The custodian, who is also a bus driver, was unavailable. Besides, I reminded myself, I am the principal. I should deal with all aspects of this school. But where does he keep that plunger?

Eventually, armed with the plunger, mop and bucket, and knee-high barn boots, I waded in and stemmed the tide. When the regular second grade teacher returned she never learned of the problem, for there was no evidence of my valiant efforts. But the custodian did ask if I knew why his barn boots were so filthy.

My assumption in the plumbing incident that "I should fix it because I'm the principal" has been echoed several times since—increasingly by others, decreasingly by me. On one such occasion the cook blustered into my office, wringing her hands about the meat sauce and the noodles and water on the floor and the funny spitting noise and the meat is all thawed and the government says we can't refreeze it and we have all that surplus cheese to use somehow and it's already 9:15—and would I please fix it right away? It did not matter to her that my desk was littered with files, computer printouts, adding machine tape, and budget requests. I went with her not because I understood the problem, but because she so obviously had one.

Actually, she had four. The steam pressure cooker was 1) not regulating itself, 2) getting threateningly hot, 3) leaking scalding water, and 4) making that funny spitting noise.

Initially she pleaded with me to "fix it before something happens." Though the problems looked and sounded worse than they actually proved, I was not ready to correct them myself, and promised to call a repairman. That did not satisfy her. Since appealing to my principalship had failed, she shifted to challenging my gender. "You're a man; fix it!"

DE NATURAE NATURA

Contrary to her assumptions, neither my profession nor my gender proves sufficient to solve all problems, especially when those problems stem from mechanical or other nonhuman sources. Mechanical problems are usually frustrating, never amusing at the time, and rarely fascinating. On the other hand, problems presented by nature are only occasionally frustrating, often amusing, and always fascinating.

Despite being a native Vermonter and having spent years hunting and fishing, I still find it singularly fulfilling to drive the fifteen minutes to school and enjoy the beginning day. Blue jays cross the road in front of my car at the same place and time each day. Cows head out to pasture. And four times in two years I have stopped the car to watch deer forage.

This may all sound rather idyllic, and it is—usually. But one spring morning a recess aide came to me to report that a cow was loose on school property. Since cows graze on adjacent meadows constantly, such trespass was not particularly noteworthy. But this aide was new, so I went with her as assurance.

The cow, however, proved to be a bull. And it was surrounded by 107 kindergarten through fourth graders, most of whom thought the whole scene quite funny. The bull obviously did not. I immediately herded the children back into the school and then set about herding the bull back to his pasture.

Not until after forty-five futile minutes of alternate pursuit and flight on my part did several staff members, trying to stifle their laughter, enlighten me that one does not herd a bull—especially an irritated bull. While performing endless, inconclusive minuets with the bull, I actually considered brandishing my jacket like a matador's cape to entice him through the gate. Fortunately for my then unestablished public image, I rejected the temptation to play El Cordobes to imaginary *Oles*! Also, fortunately for me, when the seventh graders came out for phys ed, the girl who owned the bull sauntered over, called his name, and guided him home. I thanked her, slung my cape over my shoulder, and tried to retire from the field of honor as inconspicuously as possible.

IN SEARCH OF TEETH

A less threatening natural phenomenon had me on my hands and knees on the playground, searching for a first grader's two lost teeth. They were the first teeth the child had lost, and she was heartbroken. My assurances that the Tooth Fairy was as omniscient as Santa Claus and would know what had happened even without dental evidence, did nothing to stop her tears. But my assurance that I would find her teeth worked wonders. She did not know that I caution staff members not to promise what they may not be able to deliver.

I felt a bit like an archaeologist must feel at a dig. I gently brushed sand and spread blades of grass. Five marbles, two algebra quizzes, a ring, and a chocolate chip cookie later, I found one of her teeth. One out of two was good enough for me, and I made such a show of returning it to her that one satisfied her also.

ON BEING DIPLOMATIC

Dealing with mechanical and natural disasters requires knowledge and action. Dealing with people usually requires the addition of diplomacy. During the past two years I have practiced personal diplomacy, self-defense diplomacy, and international diplomacy.

My personal diplomacy and tact are particularly tested when I counsel junior high students about sexuality. Eighth graders tend not to be as aware of or concerned about social propriety as adults, especially as it relates to "PDA"—the students' term for public display of affection. More than once I have tried to explain diplomatically and tactfully why entwined bodies at lunchtime do not mix appropriately with hot turkey sandwiches, peas, and chocolate pudding. I have tried to caution about the embarrassing, expensive, and painful consequences when two sets of braces lock in a kiss. The lovers may only become convinced that I have never been in love, but the diplomacy usually works—for a while.

One less humorous incident illustrates that even with people, knowledge and action may be the only recourse. Especially action.

As is probably the case with most principals, I have had at least one student whose behavior has been repeatedly disruptive, antisocial, and occasionally dangerous. Our discipline system involves parents as much as they are able and willing to cooperate, but one father had bucked me and the system constantly. One morning, in response to what had become a series of discipline notices, this father roared into our school parking lot via the exit, screeched to a halt in the bus loading zone, and stomped into my office demanding to see me.

I gave him time to calm down by feigning a phone call, but when I finally bade good-bye to the receiver and rose to greet him, he only became more angry. I tried to interject reason and diplomacy between his epithets and threats of everything from lawsuits to my pending need for plastic surgery. Frustrated by his failure to persuade me of the justice of his cause, the man swung his fist at my face. He missed. Before he left the building I called the police to notify them that I had been publicly threatened with personal and property injury.

At the time, this seemed to me a case where diplomacy and reason had failed completely. The next time I saw the man, however, the first thing he did was apologize for his words and actions that day.

Diplomacy on a scale more familiar to Dr. Kissinger was expected at a Halloween Party. In addition to supervising the planned extras of Halloween parties and upper-grade sports physicals, I was asked to host a group of female physicians from the People's Republic of China on the first such tour of the United States. These upper-echelon policymakers were particularly interested in rural medical service delivery systems, and would be in Vermont on Halloween. Since we had scheduled regional doctors, nurses, and interns for our school clinic that day, we were asked to serve as a whistle-stop on the Chinese tour.

It was exhilarating and humbling to consider the political and historical significance of that visit. And except for temporary confusion and panic when we had a 50 percent power failure just one hour before their scheduled arrival, the day was a joy. We spoke through interpreters and smiled a lot. The doctors seemed as interested in our school system as in our medical services, and enjoyed themselves immensely during a visit to the first grade classroom. The most difficult concept I discussed with these women had nothing to do with education or medicine. I tried vainly to explain why the children and even some teachers were dressed like Bugs Bunny, Casper the Friendly Ghost, Spider Man, Wonder Woman, and Darth Vader. In lieu of resolving that cultural dilemma, we smiled even more, posed for pictures, thanked each other, and waved good-bye.

Within fifteen minutes of their departure the business of our school day resumed. Athletes stripped to their underwear and stood on cold scales. Darth Vader and Wonder Woman worked on math at the computer. Sixth graders had a library period. And I sat in my office for a few minutes, marveling at the fascination of this job.

In my office now are two photographs that exemplify my feelings about being a principal. Though the technical and academic skills for this position come from School Finance 344, Curriculum Concepts and Development 377, and the like, the emotion comes from living it. That is the truest and most valuable training available.

One of those pictures is of five Chinese women and me. It is posed. We are dressed in our respective uniforms: suit and tie for me, blue smock-jackets and pants for the Chinese. The other photograph, also of me, is candid. I am surrounded by second graders, and in addition to my uniform I am sporting foot-tall, pink, construction-paper bunny ears and whiskers.

The key to this job is that the man in both pictures is happy.

EDWARD ROBERT WILKENS IS EMPLOYED BY NORTHEAST REGIONAL RESOURCE CENTER AND IS ENROLLED IN A DOCTORAL PROGRAM AT THE UNIVERSITY OF VERMONT.

Survival First

BARBARA L. SKIPPER

On a hot, August day four years ago I walked across the driveway of Randolph High School. Walking toward me was "Mr. Johnson," the principal, carrying a cardboard box. As we approached each other I recognized several familiar items protruding from the top of the open box. There were the pictures of his cherished wife and daughter and the box with his initials on top that usually sat on his large walnut desk. The look on his face was one of apprehension, and his eyes looked sadder than usual. Sensing that something out of the ordinary was happening, I asked, "Is there something that I need to know?" He quietly said that he had been board-approved the night before to be principal of another high school nearby. It was no secret that he and our new superintendent did not see eye-to-eye, but I still did not expect this announcement. He looked back at the school one more time and continued walking toward his car, leaving me standing in the hot sun.

I was the counselor for this secondary campus, a position I had held only one year. Mr. Johnson and I had grown close and worked well together, and I suddenly felt abandoned. I immediately headed for the superintendent's office, which was on the high school campus. I went straight to the superintendent's door without waiting for his secretary to announce me. He looked at me and said, "Do you want to be a principal?" Part of me said, "Yes!" while another part of me screamed, "NO! Not under these circumstances!" The superintendent continued talking and said that he had already contacted the five school board members who would support his recommendation of me as principal. I suddenly

60

realized that in reality it was done. I could never have imagined the roller-coaster ride that had just begun!

I entered the principal's office, which seemed barren. The hunting and fishing pictures that were still on the wall I always thought belonged to Mr. Johnson, and now I realized they belonged to an earlier principal. I left and went to my office and sat down. The registrar walked in and said, "What about registration and the master schedule?" I looked blankly back at her. She continued, "Tomorrow we will register new students and we have the master schedule to finish!" A feeling of terror instantly permeated every inch of me. I had never done a master schedule! I had visions of the first day of school with hundreds of students who had no place to go! I called the superintendent on the telephone. I told him that the master schedule needed to be completed, and I had no experience in that area. He said, "I've never done one either, but I'm sure you'll figure it out!" I truly panicked at this point.

The first lesson I learned was that the secretaries, clerks, and registrars were invaluable in "figuring out" those things that I did not know how to do. Often they needed someone to make decisions while they actually made the master schedule, registered new students, calculated attendance, and produced grade cards. Many decisions could be made with common sense and logic, relying on my previous experiences as a teacher or counselor. Sometimes simply saying, "How has this been handled before?" elicited the needed information. Since I was the only secondary principal in the district, I found that secondary principals in other districts were willing to help. In addition, the local state educational agency that provided the master scheduling, registration, and attendance software was willing to send consultants to help. It was comforting when I realized that I was truly not alone and that I did not have to know all of the answers.

In the first year there was one particularly humorous incident although the humor escaped me at the time. The event happened the first day of school. (My nightmare was coming true.) The campus had a new attendance secretary who was also responsible for assigning student lockers. She assigned students to lockers 1–300 by last name A to Z. Make sense? We thought so until half the students mutinied and ended up in my office. It seems that the TRADITION of the school was that SENIOR lockers were ALWAYS together in the English classroom hall, JUNIOR lockers were ALWAYS together in the history classroom hall, SOPHOMORE lockers were ALWAYS in the math and science classroom hall, and the FRESHMEN lockers were ALWAYS in the unpopular locker bay across from the library. I went to the hall to assess the damage and found unhappy juniors and seniors pushing and shoving their way into the locker bay to get to their lockers. They were physically too big for the narrow locker aisle and seemed to almost wedge themselves into the space. This would never work!

The second lesson that I learned was not to underestimate the ability of the students or the importance of tradition. I called the student council officers together and enlisted their help. They came up with a plan to have all students take their books to their first period class. At the end of the class, each student would put his or her books into a newly assigned locker in the proper hallway. I had my doubts about whether or not it would work but "Voila," and it was done.

I completed the year fairly successfully except for my bout with mononucleosis (great timing!) and forgetting to give tickets to the ticket takers at a football game (Post-it notes worked fine). Probably the most important lesson I learned was to keep a sense of humor! Instructional leadership took a backseat to survival that year.

BARBARA SKIPPER IS THE ASSISTANT SUPERINTENDENT IN UVALDE, TEXAS.

A Difference Runs Through Us

JAMES A. BAILEY

*A*s I sat in the darkened movie house, the line I had just heard rang in my ears so loudly I thought I would become deaf: "Why is it the ones who need the most help won't take it?" The meaning of that line rang out to me as an affirmation for my first year as principal with amazing clarity and certainty. The movie, *A River Runs Through It* continued, but I turned to the pressing matter of James.

The challenge of educating our diverse population today presents a daunting opportunity, but those of us who choose this calling are often unprepared for the difficulties that diversity poses for us. Especially challenging for me my first year was a young boy, James, and the inner struggle that I fought all year between trying to accept differences in students and pushing them toward a narrow definition of what we in school call "success."

The story of James is familiar to those of us in education: low grades, antisocial behavior, unmarried mother, poor family life, public assistance for existence. All you have to do is change the face and the name and you have the classic "at-risk" student, a label of expectation for many.

James had been in and out of our school many times when I arrived as a first year principal armed with my inner belief that all children can and will learn given the right motivation and opportunities. Unfortunately for James we never did find what it took to bring him into our vision of community. The first few months as a fifth grader, James slowly stopped working and began to get into more and more trouble. One day he was hitting people in line in the back as hard as he could; the next he was refusing to do any work; the next he was using vulgar language. Everything that his teacher and I tried seemed to push him further away from norms of acceptable behavior. According to his mother, everything could be worked out with a firmer hand. Later, on the advice of the school psychologist, we tried a softer, more humane approach letting James focus on personal issues ahead of school issues. But by mid-November, James had driven himself away from all of his classmates, had been sent to see me twenty times, and had not done anything in class in a month.

Our next step was, of course, to refer him to special education—burdening him with yet another label. Now he was not only at-risk, defiant, lazy, and a troublemaker, in our wisdom we now stuck him with the label of an emotionally disturbed eleven-year-old as if the label would cure the problem.

At first, our plan to self-contain James for most of the day worked. He connected with our special education teacher whose classroom was not so full of other people and rules. He could study what he wanted as long as he was earning time for playing the drums in the band and for computer time. He could even lounge in a beanbag to read if he wanted.

Unfortunately our optimism was premature. Within two weeks, James was back to his same behaviors—failing to work, sleeping in class, fighting—and his absences once again pronounced his hatred for school. When questioned about his absences, his mother always retorted, "Well, he's not learning that much anyway."

The moment of truth came when James was sent to see me after a fight on the playground and a bad day in class. Having worked with James in and out of class all year, I knew that using anger and power tactics would not work, yet I, like everybody else, reached my breaking point that day. When I gave James the choice of leaving until he could straighten out, he ran out of the building in a moment of brief freedom realizing, of course, that at eleven years of age he could never truly be free in an educational system based more on standardization than individuality.

Eventually, James was placed in an adolescent psychiatric ward where nothing was found to be wrong. When he returned to us, he was put back into the regular classroom on a strict behavioral plan. James left us for good in late April after an emotional outburst when he told me he could not go back into any classroom again. He called his social worker and within a few minutes his mother ran into school. Instead of consoling him, she yanked him up by the hair and took him back to the psychiatric ward. Like the rest of us, she was acting in frustration and looking for answers outside of herself.

In the end, James's mother approached us with a home schooling plan to prepare James for sixth grade. She promised that he would study and learn and be a better kid next year because there would be a different set of teachers and this was just one of those years. I never got too optimistic as I would drive by his house day after day hoping to see him reading, talking with another adult or building something in his front yard. In fact, all I ever saw was James sitting on the curb tossing pebbles into the stream of water floating by in the gutter probably wishing he could go where the water took him.

Rewatching the end of *A River Runs Through It* months later, I am reminded that as a beginning principal the ideals of human life and happiness far exceed the narrow need to succeed academically. Acceptance and acknowledgment of people's differences is the first and only step toward the larger end: learning to live. One of the ending quotes from the movie is, "In the end all things converge, and a river runs through it." If this movie had been about James, the end quote might have been, "In the end we all converge to one ideal, but a river of difference runs through us."

JAMES A. BAILEY IS THE PRINCIPAL AT DARRELL SMITH HIGH SCHOOL IN STERLING, COLORADO.

The Chocolate Milk Compromise

ANITA PAGE

I wasn't their first choice. In fact, I was their fourth choice. In late August, I received a phone call from the superintendent of a rural school district where I had interviewed in the spring. Their first and second choices had declined the job offer; an interim arrangement with a teacher in the school had fallen through. Would I come in for another interview?

If I knew then what I know now after twelve years as a school principal, I would have picked up my bag and run in the opposite direction after that meeting with him. The superintendent was very frank. The school had had a new principal every two or three years. My immediate predecessor had been pressured to leave by the school committee, and the teacher who offered to serve in the interim was not welcomed by the other teachers. After the meeting, he offered me the position and I took it without knowing any better.

School opened without me because I had to meet a deadline on my dissertation proposal. At the first meeting with the teachers, it was clear that they saw me as a bird of passage. After all, they had lived through many principals. All of the teachers had been at the school more than ten years.

It was a unique school. Its funding was high because of the taxes from a nuclear power plant in the town, and the town itself was the most prosperous in a poor county. Three-quarters of its students were tuitioned in from the next town, the poorest one in the county. All students received free lunches, classes did not exceed sixteen in number, and the school owned enough cross-country skis to equip every single student.

I was on my own in a rural district twenty-five miles from the district office. So if any emergency happened, I had to deal with it on the spot. The previous principal had left me no background information or suggestions. I spent the first few weeks trying to inform myself by reading two years of school committee minutes, and every other piece of paper I could lay my hands on. Essentially, I left the teachers alone.

I had not come well prepared for the principalship. I had been a drama teacher, an arts coordinator, and had become certified at a time when only one supervision course was required. What stood me in good stead was my theatre directing experience where I learned how to work with groups and how to develop talent. And I was good at improvising.

What I did not understand then is that there are certain elements of a school culture—the sacred cows—that must not be changed without great care, if at all. The kitchen of the school was one such element. The school committee took pride in the fact that they could afford to give free lunches to all children and had a cook who made delicious desserts served with chocolate milk. She played a central, nurturing role in the school. The lunches were a symbol of abundance in an area of scarcity. I frankly was concerned about the amount of sugar being consumed during the day (including morning snacks), and by the end of my first month I declared that we would serve only white milk. If I had said we would do a sun dance around the school every morning, I could not have stirred up a greater fuss. I ended up with a compromise: we would alternate white and chocolate milk. What I learned from that experience was the necessity to examine the role that certain practices play in a school. If you feel they need to be changed for educational or health reasons, you need to find a substitute for the symbolic role that that practice has served.

I learned that communicating with parents is also a learned art. A number of the parents did not understand some of the progressive practices of the school, such as not correcting every spelling error in the first draft of a child's writing, because they were different from their own schooling experiences. When parents came in to ask about spelling in students' first drafts, I was quick to launch into a defense of what we were doing. After some counterproductive parent meetings, I learned that a number of these people were not protesting what we were doing but wanted a chance to express their confusion about what we were doing. What they wanted more than anything else was an opportunity to make their perceptions known. In that year, I learned that good communication with parents means not only informing them of what you are doing, but also listening to them and keeping the door open.

Some of the staff and some of the community members were more understanding of my goals in education than others. I had no central office staff nearby or fellow principals to turn to. So I did turn to certain staff and certain community members for support. I learned, however, that you must seek that kind of support with discretion. I generated some resentment among staff and community members who felt they weren't in "my camp." Although a principal must find support in the school, she is ultimately the principal of the entire community and needs to project that primary responsibility.

After four years, I left that position for a larger school in a college town, definitely with a feeling of goodwill and a sense of accomplishment. That first year was a crash course in school change, parent relations, and diplomacy. It only took four years in my new position to get a salad bar introduced in the cafeteria!

ANITA PAGE IS THE PRINCIPAL OF MOSIER ELEMENTARY SCHOOL IN SOUTH HADLEY, MASSACHUSETTTS.

Worth the Sacrifice

JANE C. SHIPP

As I look back on my first year as the head of an independent school, I would characterize it as one of ups and downs to a degree unusual in my experience. Several crises occurred that would have been more than challenging for an old pro, crises which (for legal reasons) I cannot describe even after three years. There were other extremes as well: mood swings ranging from unexpected joy in accomplishments to discouragement over problems that seemed insoluble. There were occasions when I practically broke my arm patting myself on the back, and others when I felt certain I was in the wrong profession. And these two sentiments would occur in the same twenty-four hour period, leaving me slightly schizophrenic.

I marvel now that I had the energy to sustain my momentum through that first year. When I think of the organizational changes that I put into place while trying to get to know at least a thousand new people, making my way in a new community, earning the respect of a hundred employees of the school, and attending to the myriad daily details that are routine for all of us, I don't know how I did it, and I wonder whether I could do it again.

On second thought, I know that I was able to do it because of the support I was lucky enough to find from so many individuals and groups of people in the school community. I was blessed with an exceptionally good president of the board of trustees who gave me just the right amount of support and advice and provided just the right amount of autonomy for me. The faculty and staff were eager for a new era and did not block any of the changes that I needed to make. Indeed, they gave me wholehearted support as I plunged into deep water. Nevertheless, I came to learn in that first year the price I pay for maintaining an appropriate level of comfort and civility in the interactions over which I preside. I am collaborative and democratic to a fault, which is a time-consuming modus operandi. Because I believe so completely in the value of an inclusive process of decision making, I don't feel successful merely having made a decision; I feel successful only when I have persuaded others to engage themselves in the outcome of that decision. Such an expectation for success is draining.

It also became clear to me that I am not able to keep my hands out of the details of running a school. I like to choose the color of the paint; I want to do all the teacher evaluations; I try to know all five hundred children's names; I attend faculty and trustee committee meetings and parent association meetings. The list is long. This approach is probably not sensible for the long term, and it undoubtedly accounts for the unreasonable hours that I spend at school and the board's fear that I will "burn out." I know I should change these habits, but I face the fact that my compulsiveness is not only an integral part of my personality, but also responsible to some degree for whatever success I've had. Now as I begin year number four and a capital campaign looms ahead, I know I won't be able to continue this level of involvement. Learning to delegate more effectively will be a major challenge.

I was startled that first year, and have continued to be surprised, by the degree of affection that I have received from all sides. Without it I would not function as well, and I continue to be grateful that it happens. I doubt that I could work for any length of time in an adversarial environment, although many school heads do. I learned early on that it is an immense joy to structure situations so that everybody comes out winning. When I can make that happen, I'm elated. I have a high tolerance for eccentricity and even for cantankerous behavior, as long as it serves the common good and ultimately benefits the children. Given the culture of my school, it is fortunate that I have this tolerance. It is a trick and a half to maintain one's own integrity and the integrity of one's vision for the school in such a culture, but with patience and care it can be done—and what a glorious feeling when it all comes together!

I remember many accomplishments from my first year: putting into place a fair and open salary system; establishing a preliminary faculty evaluation procedure; setting up a structure of faculty and staff committees to participate in decision making; preparing the school's first curriculum guide for parents; organizing the process for developing a strategic plan; reworking the progress report forms and procedure; rebuilding a sense of trust on the part of parents in the school and its mission. I often pondered, during that time and afterward, the right and wrong use of power in a position such as mine.

Heads have power, no doubt about it, though not as much as most people think. It was a shock to me to realize how much of the job is reactive. It seems to me I have mended more than my share of fences that should not have been broken in the first place. Particularly in the beginning, I felt as if I were constantly reacting to other people's stimuli, which is apt to leave one feeling ever so slightly out of control!

I remind myself, when I need to, that the power we heads have is the power to do good; that is why people like us take on headships. In addition, I have been sustained always by the conviction that the work I do is important work, the most important work in the world. When I'm particularly tired or discouraged, I ask myself whether it's work that is worth sacrificing such a huge amount of one's personal life for: I also wonder about the ego of someone who answers that question, as I do: "Yes! What I can accomplish here is worth the cost." Nevertheless, I said that at the end of my first year and I still say it. I know that I am privileged to have an opportunity as rich as that of heading a school. Now if only I can raise salaries, keep the budget balanced, reach the annual fund goal, take care of deferred maintenance, help the board stay appropriately engaged, maintain faculty morale, hear parents' concerns, and be sure the students learn what they should—then I will sleep well at night.

JANE C. SHIPP IS THE HEADMISTRESS OF THE RENBROOK SCHOOL IN WEST HARTFORD, CONNECTICUT.

Entry: The Door to Effective Headship

ALBERT M. ADAMS

I have had the good fortune to experience *two* first years as a school head—the first as I began my five-year tenure at the Cambridge School of Weston, and the second, when I arrived at Lick-Wilmerding in 1988. As I approached each of these "new beginnings," well-intentioned friends offered conventional advice: "Enjoy the honeymoon." "Spend the first year listening." Others, in contradiction, intoned, "Think of the first hundred days of the presidency; put yourself on the map early with dramatic initiatives."

While these exhortations contained elements of wisdom, I instinctively knew that any, taken literally, was bad advice. My instincts were confirmed when, six months before moving to Weston, I was introduced to Barry Jentz and the book, *Entry*, which he coauthored with his partner, Joan Wofford. Written primarily for public school superintendents and principals, *Entry* suggests a fresh and dynamic process for assuming leadership at a new school—namely to enter, in equal measures, as anthropologist and proactive leader. It offers a practical solution to the conundrum with which a head of school struggles: how to start, and particularly, how to balance the need to listen and learn with the need to assert strong leadership.

An underlying premise of *Entry* is that I, as the arriving head, am entering my new school with respect—that is, without preconceptions or pet prescriptions for what the school ought to become. Another is that it is not *my* school; instead my role is that of leader

72

and steward for one important chapter in the school's evolution, with connection, continuity, and change being the threads that stitch together past, present, and future. Another premise predates, but seems to anticipate, Peter Senge's notion of the "learning organization," with *inquiry, reflection, and growth* being at the center of the enterprise. *Entry* also allows me, as the new head, to incorporate Lee Bolman's and Terry Deal's four "frames" through which to view an organization. Specifically, it provides the discipline to assure that I look equally through the structural, human resource, political, and symbolic lenses. Further, the very act of modeling my respect for the community and my commitment to honest inquiry is a symbolic statement that can define my entire tenure at the school.

When I started as head at Lick-Wilmerding, my public commitment was to spend an hour to an hour and a half with each board member and administrator prior to September, and with each faculty member before Thanksgiving. In addition, I would do the same with representative samples of parents, students and alumni/ae—mostly individually, but sometimes in small groups.

My introductory letter to the various constituencies included my reasons for undertaking this formal entry process, the timetable for feedback/validation sessions (late fall), a projection of planning steps, and the list of questions that would form the backbone of the semi-structured interview format I would use in our upcoming conversations. My letter spoke of the special opportunity I wanted to seize to fill in the portrait of Lick which I was painting in my mind. It went on to say that, "I want to take advantage of this transitional moment—to capture the freshness of early insights, to appreciate the various angles of vision and to understand the issues which define Lick's hopes and challenges for the future."

Beyond communicating to the entire community what kinds of inquiries I would make in the interviews, inclusion of the questions with the introductory letter allowed interviewees to prepare answers, if they chose. Many, in fact, came with pages of notes, and a few even submitted well-developed papers. In addition to several inquiries about personal stories and points of connection with Lick, I also posed questions such as:

- What are the key issues facing Lick today? Why is each important? Can you rank these issues in priority order?
- What qualities do you most want to see preserved at Lick-Wilmerding?
- What networks of people are typically interested in influencing decision making? What do the members of these networks have in

common? How do they differ?

· Describe a moment when the school was in conflict. How did the conflict arise? What people or groups played roles in it? How? How was the problem resolved? Might it have been handled differently?

· Describe a difficult decision you have had to make (as a board member). Why was it important? How did you reach your decision? What did others think? Would you, in retrospect, have done anything differently?

The public nature of the plan was, in itself, a powerful statement to the community about how I intended to do business. In addition to signaling an open and inclusive leadership style, my questions reflected the seriousness, breadth, and depth that would characterize my initial inquiries, as well as my ongoing approach to leadership at Lick.

Certainly one immediate and pragmatic result of announcing my *Entry* intentions was that every "key player" was assured of equal access to "my ear." This notion of establishing a "level playing field" right from the start has paid significant dividends throughout these five years. On the more personal, less political side, nothing convinces people of your genuine interest in them better than focused, uninterrupted one-on-one time. Amazingly, I can think of a dozen examples from the academic year just past when one colleague or another made reference to our initial conversation five years ago! The impact of those first six months not only set the stage for our work together, but has endured in dramatic and surprising ways.

The explicit purpose of *Entry* is to identify prevalent themes that define the school of today, including any major challenges that require attention. In many cases it is recurring stories, rather than specific information, that provide the deepest insights. In addition, the new head also begins to learn about the personal and political forces at play as he/she begins to fashion strategies for moving the school forward.

The real power of *Entry* is that it puts the new head in a position to say, in effect, to each constituency: "Here is what you (in the aggregate, since all individual perspectives are confidential) have told me. Did I get it right? Given these insights and perspectives, here is how I believe we should proceed." The resulting opportunity to refer continually to "what you have told me" and "my understanding of how you view it" allows the head to enjoy many of the benefits of being a consultant—that is, to take the high road, while also being the most central participant.

A magical moment in my entry to Lick came in late August of that first summer when the board joined us for a working session at our faculty retreat.

The goal was to write individually, then in small groups, and last as a whole group, a one-paragraph mission statement for the school. Having achieved that, we pushed to the next level of distilling the essence of the "ideal Lick" into short metaphorical banners or mottoes. The central issues and descriptive languages which emerged came directly out of the first two months of *Entry* interviews! What is more, those foundations: "EDUCATION FOR THE HEAD, HEART, HANDS," "PRIVATE SCHOOL WITH PUBLIC PURPOSE," "CAN-DO CONFIDENCE" have resonated with every constituency, including alums from sixty and seventy years ago, with whom I have met over these five years. They also became the central elements of the strategic plan and financial long-range plan which we developed over the next two years. In a very literal way the issues, ideas, and language that bubbled up in the entry process have become Lick-Wilmerding's anchor—the summation of past virtues, present achievements, and future dreams.

A final premise underlying the theory of *Entry* is that it represents the beginning of a systematic, ongoing planning process. Thus, at the end of my first year at Lick, with *Entry* wrapped in tidy bows, we had Susan Stone, a strategic planner, facilitate the beginning of a full review of the school's goals, rationales, and implementation steps for all twelve components of an independent school. The process which followed unfolded over the next eight months, and we published a twenty-four page document which included a financial long-range plan, with five-year projections.

These steps are relevant in the context of *Entry* because the fundamental building blocks surfaced and were crystallized in those first six months: quality of program (top salaries and benefits), full integration of the technical arts (shops) into the rigorous college prep curriculum, access, and affordability (to assure that students of color and students paying "flexible tuition" represent at least a third of the school). They became a credo of sorts—a regular expression and affirmation of our shared values. As such, they serve as both prod and measuring stick, and their enduring effectiveness derives from the knowledge that they truly have their roots in the soul of the whole community.

ALBERT ADAMS IS THE HEADMASTER AT LICK-WILMERDING HIGH SCHOOL IN SAN FRANCISCO, CALIFORNIA.

Baptism by Fire

JUDITH T. HORNBECK

*Y*ou have heard of baptism by fire? Well, consider a baptism that included fire, floods, contaminated water, a bomb threat, and an asbestos removal accident requiring total evacuation of the school. Not only was my desire to become a principal severely tested, but my very faith itself!

I left a position as the assistant principal of a middle school in a neighboring county to assume the principalship of a K–5 school, housing approximately six hundred students. I assumed my duties midyear with the knowledge that the school was undergoing extensive remodeling, including many areas of new construction. During my intensive interview sessions, I was also made aware of the school community's desire for a strong, visionary leader, who would be called upon to solve the school's multiple problems as quickly as possible. Interestingly enough, ownership of a magic wand was never mentioned as a job requirement!

My first two days passed in a deceptively calm manner. I met more than sixty staff members and started playing the name game! I visited classrooms, was interviewed by members of the press, and was feeling pretty pleased with myself. Then . . . Day 3 arrived. An innocent holiday door decorating contest spawned my first calamity. One of the kindergarten teachers had used angels as part of the holiday decorations. Heaven Forbid! After solving the "angel flap" dilemma and drying the teacher's tears, I was propelled rapidly into Day 5, which opened with a bus accident. Although no one was seriously injured, the entire community was shaken by the event that received extensive press coverage. (Not exactly the headlines I had hoped for!)

An eternal optimist, I started Week 2 with a clean slate. My bliss, however, was short-lived. Friday afternoon, I was called home to check on a potential furnace fire. Shortly after I left, a fire erupted in a transformer on the school roof! There was no structural damage and no injuries, but I could sense the first tremors of faltering faith.

Several weeks sped by as I adjusted to my new environment. Always an early bird, I arrived early and stayed late, often working twelve- or fourteen-hour days. I began to flex my leadership muscles as teachers began coming to me with educational problems and concerns. Ah, the lull before the storm.

After a particularly heavy winter rainstorm, I arrived at school early one Monday to find the front section of the auditorium under three feet of water! The construction workers had blocked the egress for the storm drains. The superintendent arrived to take a look, and the problem was "fixed." Imagine my surprise when the entire scenario was repeated again, this time on a Saturday morning—I just happened to stop by the school because I was concerned by the heavy downpour. Needless to say, this time the problem was permanently fixed.

During this entire time period, I had become extremely popular with the construction crew, the job foreman, the clerk of the works, and the school engineer. Actually, they tried to hide when they saw me coming! Renovation of a school with the students still present is difficult at best, and despite these problems, I really did have a good rapport with the construction crew.

Spring finally arrived only to bring additional water woes. We survived two separate incidents with impure water, one due to the presence of E-coli bacteria, the other resulting from rust and sediment contamination. The entire school drank bottled water from water coolers placed strategically around the school.

Time for another full-scale evacuation! I received a bomb threat through our in-school postal system, WEE DELIVER. The police were called and the building was dutifully searched and pronounced "safe." Students patiently filed back into the building and resumed their day. One teacher mentioned the real possibility that the school was "jinxed!" (I have received several four-leaf clovers as presents!)

Everyone is familiar with the old saying, "Save the best for last." I will never forget the feeling I had the day the engineer came to my office to tell me that a construction worker had accidentally disturbed some floor tiles that could contain asbestos. I determined that we needed not only to evacuate immediately, but that we needed to send the children home until scientific tests could be completed. Again, I was a media star. Three local television stations arrived, all clamoring for an interview. I received the "all-clear" sign that night, and we returned to school the next day.

Throughout my first year as principal, I received overwhelming support from staff, parents, and students. I found that there is a special spirit of enthusiastic cooperation in school that cannot be duplicated anywhere else. Although I received numerous gifts at the end of the year, none could compare to the words of thanks I received from my staff for guiding them through a most difficult and trying year. . . . Now, where did I put that magic wand?

JUDITH HORNBECK IS THE PRINCIPAL OF T. C. WALKER ELEMENTARY SCHOOL IN GLOUCESTER, VIRGINIA.

Adversity: It's Our Reward?

JOHN R. KELLY

*E*ven though my first year as principal was thirteen years ago, many of the days during that year stand out vividly in my memory. It was a year that taught me an incredible amount about schools, their organization, and the politics of organizations.

The advertisements for the principal position were published in late July. I was aware that the town of Leduc had established its own Catholic school district the previous year. My wife had a passing acquaintance with one of the newly elected trustees, and, knowing that I was a teacher, he would occasionally pass on information to her about the problems they were having in establishing their district. When I saw the ad, I figured I would throw in an application for the position.

I was only thirty at the time. The six years teaching experience I had gave me a sense that administration might be a possibility. Somehow the thought of being in charge of a school appealed to me. At any rate, in July of 1990, I assembled my resumé and sent it off.

Within a week, I got a call. I met with an area superintendent for Edmonton Catholic Schools who had taken on the position in Leduc as sort of a lend-lease arrangement. He explained to me that the board hoped to begin operations in September with a bus load of students coming into Edmonton (approximately 20 km) while awaiting the construction of the board's first school, which was slated to open the following September. The board, he claimed, wanted to get things rolling slowly so that the school opening could be smooth. They had already hired a teacher for the kindergarten program (which was to be run in the church basement in Leduc) and another teacher for the middle grades. Classroom space was secured for us, he claimed, in an underused elementary school in Edmonton.

It all sounded great to me. With the wide-eyed enthusiasm of a true rookie, I expounded on my theories of education, discipline, and religion. He must have been impressed, because two days later I got a call to meet with the board the next week for a formal interview.

When that evening came around, I had a chance to shake hands with the other applicant on his way out. He was about fifteen years older than I and was introduced as Doctor somebody. I figured the game was over. I was just being brought in to fill out the slate. With nothing to lose, I let the trustees (one gentleman was away on holidays) have both barrels. We joked, talked, planned, and dreamed together. For over an hour and a half, all the world seemed to stand still as we envisioned the future successes of the yet to be named, yet to be built, yet to be opened school.

Lo and behold, the next morning I got the phone call. The board loved me. Would I take the job? The answer was an immediate affirmative. Monday would be my starting day. After all, we only had two weeks to go before school was supposed to open and there would certainly be a lot to do.

So many things happened in rapid succession during those last two weeks of August that my head still spins. In no particular order, they were:

- No, we would not bus the kids into Edmonton after all. Instead, portable classrooms would be located on our school site, supposedly within the first month of the school year.
- Yes, the parents in town loved the idea of no busing to the city, so twice as many students registered as had been expected.
- The trustee who was away on holidays came back and was aghast that the board had hired a principal without his opinion being considered. Over the next ten months, he was to be a personal thorn in my side. This was despite the fact that a) we shared the same last name, and b) he was a teacher with the city district.
- At the first regularly scheduled board meeting after my appointment, the secretary-treasurer (also on loan from the city district) stormed out of the room and resigned because of my namesake's antics.
- I was authorized to hire another teacher to meet our rapidly expanding enrollment. When I interviewed the first applicant for the job, she broke down in tears, explaining that she just found out that she was pregnant, and her wedding was only a week away. I figured that she

was honest and had courage, so I hired her.

· The board decided to name the school Notre Dame. Also, while we waited for the portables to be moved from the city, we contracted to use Sunday school facilities of the local Pentecostal church. They were far below school standards, but they would only be for a few weeks, we were assured.

· My staff and I had to begin the task of assembling a school overnight from scratch. Since we were the only school in the district, there was no one to lean on for help. Our students were coming out of the town's public school system, so colleagues in the system were understandably cool toward us. We had no supplies, no textbooks, no furniture, no curriculum guides, no forms to fill out, and no policy manual for operations.

Somehow, in those two weeks, we put together a school. The day after Labor Day students arrived, all fresh and clean, ready for a new experience in a new school system. We opened with ninety students in grades one through six and another twenty-five in kindergarten. The board was elated. Things were under way. Our problems had just begun.

Running an elementary school out of Sunday-school rooms in the basement of a church would have been fine if it was just for a month. The promise of portables was not as easy as it seemed. We were not able to move in until the week before Christmas. Every Friday, we had to put all our belongings away in a storage room and move the chairs, tables, and walls back to their original position. Each Monday, we had to do the reverse.

The euphoria of opening a new school quickly turned into the routine of any September. Along toward the end of the month, one of the staff inquired, "When do we get paid?" This brought on a wonderful exercise in innovation. No one had thought about how payroll was to be set up, what procedures were to be followed, or which wage scale we were to follow (each school district in the province negotiates independently with its own board). With the help of our provincial teachers' association, a contract settlement was reached with our board.

With no central office, a superintendent for only two days a month, and a rather unique group of school trustees, school operations were a challenge and a joy. We wrote school policy as things happened. It was both a principal's dream and nightmare.

Our students were generally not the scholars from the other school district, so we had to set up a resource room program. I got to interview and hire the teacher. Unfortunately, the Provincial Department of Education decided, a month after we had hired her, that her credentials from New Zealand did not qualify her to teach in Alberta. We went on a two-year appeal process to have one of the most talented teachers I have ever encountered keep her job.

We also hired and fired substitute teachers and janitors. We had our first maternity leave and an intervention by the Social Services Department on a child neglect case. Throughout everything, an excellent staff and supportive parents kept the school operating. The new building was begun in February. Our enrollments increased monthly. I made my share of rookie mistakes but had successes, too. Things were sailing along fine until late April. Then, the crisis came.

During the course of the school year my namesake on the board had been causing all sorts of problems. Being a teacher himself (you can sit as a trustee in Alberta if you do not teach in the district, but only reside there), he figured that he knew education pretty well. He was close to retirement age and had emigrated from Scotland only ten years before. As human beings go, he was the most disagreeable individual I have ever met.

Our number projections for September showed us having nearly three hundred students. The superintendent and I estimated that we would need at least a dozen new staff members. His instructions to me were simple: solicit applications, interview candidates, and come to the board with a proposed staff list. I did as I was instructed. It was a wonderful part of the job to talk with teachers about building a school district together. My trustee friend, however, did not think it was proper procedure for a young principal to make hiring decisions and forward them directly to the board.

In late April, at a private board meeting, the superintendent and my trustee friend squared off in a shouting match. They hurled accusations back and forth like snowballs. After one particularly fierce volley, the superintendent slammed his briefcase shut, said he had another meeting in the city, and stormed out of the room, leaving me alone with five trustees and a recommended staff list. Somehow I got out of the meeting alive.

The next morning, I was summoned to the superintendent's office in Edmonton to discuss our next course of action. He informed me that he was going to offer a letter of resignation and wondered if I was going to do the same. His logic was simple: The chairman of the board would have a choice of us or one of his trustees. Which direction did he want the school district to take? I was looking down the barrel of a loaded gun. I needed the job, the superintendent was merely on loan. Summoning up all the courage I could muster, I wrote a letter too. Together, we presented them to the chairman and waited. By midnight we were informed that three trustees had resigned and by-election papers would be issued the next morning to fill the vacancies. We had won.

The year ended with sunshine, final exams, and class trips. Our new building was being built before our very eyes. Everyone had a collective sense that we had survived a rather unique first year. The school operates today with a strong spirit of community togetherness. Although I left after the third year, some of my founding staff are still teaching there and still tell the stories from that first year. Adversity is often its own reward.

JOHN KELLY TEACHES AT ST. ALBERT HIGH SCHOOL IN ST. ALBERT, ALBERTA.

The Leap Year of 1992

MARK KAVARSKY

I was fortunate that it was a leap year. I was hired in February 1992 as the interim acting principal of Salome Urena de Henriquez Intermediate School 218 in the Washington Heights–Inwood section of upper Manhattan. IS 218 was scheduled to open on March 2, 1992. Therefore, I had just one month to make a vision into a reality. Leap year provided me with a much-needed extra day.

The challenges before me were formidable. IS 218 was the first of many new schools planned by the New York City School Construction Authority in District Six. The middle school was the first new school under construction in more than twenty years for a neighborhood struggling with the city's most overcrowded schools, a large population of poor, first-generation immigrant families, many young people at risk of dropping out of school, and not enough assistance from the city's large service providers. It was also a community with a drive to succeed. Members of the community were determined to help their children despite the absence of medical, dental, and health services and a strong presence of drugs. Recognizing the urgent need for services, the concept of a "community school" was developed.

The community school would be an integral part of the community and contain all of the health and welfare services of a large social service agency under the roof of IS 218. It would serve as a focal point to which children and their parents could turn for both education and all those social services they sorely needed.

Suddenly and without warning, the role of the principal evolved from the educational leader of a school to the facilitator of the community school. At the same time, the work of the principalship evolved from a seven-hour and twenty-minute workday into a six-days-a-week, fifteen-hours-a-day, year-round schedule.

What was proposed was not just to use the school from 3:00 to 10:00 P.M. every day, but to work side by side with the parents, health agencies, and community-based organizations to ensure that children had every chance to succeed. Consequently, the construction of the school had to be modified to accommodate such a concept. I worked tirelessly with the School Construction Authority, not only to complete their construction in a timely fashion for the March opening, but also to make adjustments in the original blueprints to create a family resource room, a parenting resource room, a medical and dental services room, and a health and social services room. Hours of meetings ensued as medical and health service agencies as well as the local community-based organizations met with me to collaborate on plans for the opening of IS 218. Fortunately, the Children's Aid Society joined the collaboration to provide medical, dental, and health services to the community. The expertise and resources of C.A.S. made a dream into a reality by June of 1992. Even Mercy College joined the collaboration to offer degree-bound credit and continuing education courses to the mothers and fathers of our children both in the day and in the evening at IS 218.

The recruitment of staff was only partially completed by February 1992. District Six had completed an agreement with the union stating that one-third of the staff would be acquired through a seniority application plan outside of District Six, and one-third of the staff would be acquired through principal's choice. In reality, few teachers could obtain easy approval in the month of February (middle of the school year) from either their district and/or principal to transfer to a new school.

Moreover, I had difficulty convincing teachers with experience to transfer to a school district notorious for overcrowded and decaying facilities. My repeated attempts to recruit a quality work force were especially frustrating as I spent long hours on the telephone each night trying to convince the large pool of excellent teachers to take a risk. The more I spoke of a "community school" concept, however, the less favorable was the reaction of my colleagues. It became obvious to me that the majority of teachers would rather remain in a known setting despite the adversities, than transfer to an unknown setting that could potentially make their professional dreams come true. I would remember this lesson as I planned the organizational structure of the school.

One week before the opening of the school, the administrators, teachers, paraprofessionals, aides, and parent volunteers were in place. The Children's Aid Society and C.B.O.'s were hard at work soliciting funding for their services. Endless hours of cabinet meetings helped to formulate a mission statement for the school. IS 218 would soon become Salome Urena Middle Academies (SUMA). In 1991, I had earned my Ed.D. from Fordham University by studying the most successful middle schools in and around the metropolitan New York City area. I was convinced that an inner-city school could obtain positive results by utilizing a middle school philosophy.

Consequently, IS 218 with a student population of twelve hundred students was transformed into four sub-schools (academies) with a population of approximately three hundred students. Each academy would be self-autonomous with teams of teachers making decisions to meet the needs of the teachers, parents, and children that they governed. An opportunity to collaborate and reflect on decisions was provided for each team with the intent to create a professional working environment. Staff development was emphasized with before, during, and after school workshops on middle school philosophy, discipline with dignity, advisories, curriculum development, theme infusion, flexible scheduling, and interdisciplinary planning. We offered brainstorming and consensus-building courses and encouraged people to take risks.

My last task was to develop a school climate that recognized the characteristics of the middle school child. Dramatic changes in the physical, emotional, and cognitive growth of early adolescents warranted an instructional program that facilitated the new capacity to think in more abstract and complex ways. Teams of teachers began to plan interdisciplinary themes that encouraged children to work cooperatively and on long-term projects using a hierarchy of critical thinking skills.

Because the middle school child has an increased sense of self and an enhanced capacity for intimate relationships with both adults and peers, an advisory program was established in which every child has an adult mentor and a small group of classmates to turn to in times of need. The overall effect of educating the "whole child" has been the community's acceptance of the school as a caring home and safe haven. Not surprisingly, nearly 50 percent of our children voluntarily remain in our extended day programs rather than return to their mean streets.

The result of the efforts of many individuals at SUMA speaks for itself. In a few short months, SUMA staff have already received invitations to speak at local, state, and national forums on such varied topics as community youth service for the middle school child and the integration of the "community school" concept and curriculum. A thirty-minute documentary on SUMA titled "Three O'Clock and Beyond" has been broadcast by PBS. The children of SUMA have been featured on the cover of *Middle School Years* and written about in many local and national newspapers and journals. The parents and the community have forged a compact with their "community school" that has set a model for schools of the twenty-first century.

Upon reflection, I have never worked harder in my life than I have worked in my first year as a principal. Nevertheless, I look forward to future leap years with the knowledge that I will once again have a much-needed extra day.

MARK KAVARSKY IS PRINCIPAL AT INTERMEDIATE SCHOOL 218 IN NEW YORK CITY.

Not Quite a Noble Example

SCOTT D. THOMSON

*S*uddenly, it struck my consciousness with the force of a tidal wave. On the first day of school, as students streamed from the initial back-to-school group orientation and headed for the classrooms, I realized there was nothing I could do now that would make a difference. As principal, I was supposed to be leading, to be in charge, but already events had streaked beyond my control.

Yes, I had been on the job and "in control" for two months, meeting with faculty and arranging for September's opening activities. I felt confident that school would begin smoothly. But, as the students moved from the bleachers, my confidence was overwhelmed by a sense of vulnerability. The events of the balance of the day, and to a large degree of the entire year, were beyond my direct control. School had begun to move forward to its rendezvous with June, and I was simply a ghost conductor, my baton hidden from most of the players most of the time. If teachers and students chose to mangle the composition, I feared, then it would be clear evidence of the incompetence of the new principal. My fate as a principal, therefore, depended in large measure on the wisdom and experience and goodwill of others in the school, and on my ability to shape these attributes in a program beneficial to all on campus. This job of leadership was more complicated than I had envisioned.

I walked back to my office with assistant principals Bill Hutchinson and Phyllis Leveen, sat down at the desk, and stared at the appointment calendar. It was blank, offering mute evidence of my expendability. The train was moving, and nobody wanted to talk to the engineer.

Then I glanced again at the calendar, dated Monday, September 14, 1964, and knew that I would be all right. Printed on the bottom of the page was Bert Estabrook's observation that "One needs common sense to succeed, and a sense of humor to be happy." Assuredly I have these qualities, I thought, and so, feeling better, turned the calendar to Tuesday. Four appointments and a meeting had been printed neatly by my secretary. Perhaps I could be useful after all.

Nine and a half months and 180 school days later brought graduation for the seniors of Cubberley High School. Some observers contend that graduation ceremonies are for parents and not for the students who would settle for a simple diploma. Actually, graduation is for new principals, as well. It provides visible affirmation for the principal of the significance of the job, and it offers personal assurances of worth seldom found in other occupations.

Whatever else happens during that first year, the successes and the defeats and the inconsequentials, graduation stands firm as the closing gate. It also is the preeminent public ritual in American culture, a summit experience for parents and families. Graduation offers discernible evidence of a continuing national rebirth generationally, intellectually, socially, and economically. It provides the keystone of continuity for the American culture as expressed in the late twentieth century. The family continues, the occupations flourish, and the community and nation grow. Without schooling and its capstone ceremony over which principals preside, the national welfare would erode.

At these graduation ceremonies, new as well as veteran principals are the visible, front-stage symbols of the entire event. They represent the faculty and its work and the achievements of students. And they affirm that the young people crossing the stage may now be called adults. Symbolically, this is major league, with the principal standing at its center. For the first-year principal, this is heady stuff, nourishing the spirit beyond whatever bruises and doubts remain from the mistakes of inexperience. Yes, graduation is for principals as well as for parents.

I have kept the appointment calendar from my first year as principal and find the initial entries enlightening in retrospect. The first contacts in July are a diverse lot: a meeting with the superintendent, a Rotary Club luncheon, conferences with the assistant principals and the P.T.A. president, interviews with teacher candidates for a late vacancy, and a briefing from the chair of our tech prep committee, a program again popular in the 1990s.

Then the teachers with agendas drifted in, one by one. First came Dave Buck, the drama teacher who wanted to gauge my interest in the arts. Then two department chairs appeared seeking redress for budget decisions made earlier. They were followed by Gypsy Laurence, the social studies aide with work-load concerns; by Sylvia Hoyt, a liberal English teacher who thought the curriculum restrictive; and by Dottie Bradshaw, another English teacher with whom my wife and I shared mutual friends. Soon thereafter arrived a reporter from the Palo Alto *Times* and the director of buildings and grounds for the school district with the veiled message that his staff, and not the building custodians, were to conduct all maintenance.

As a new principal, confident that my progressive ideas about improving instruction and delegating major responsibilities to teachers would be received warmly, I began to understand that my agenda for the school was only one of many. Furthermore, some agendas had long roots leading back for years, confirming that teachers possess long memories that are activated when new principals appear. Clearly, if my agenda was to gain broad support, then I must show consideration for these problems. Contrary to the view that new principals enjoy a honeymoon of six months in which to act, I believe that old hurts and issues should be addressed early as they arise, if only to listen and discuss. Then teachers will be motivated to support the principal's program. A proper courtship must precede the honeymoon if the marriage is going to work in the long run.

The question of expectations faces all principals. How do your expectations for teachers and students square with those of the school culture? Is the school driven to excel by tradition or by the professionalism of key teachers, or is morale flat with little sign of group standards? Do students feel they should live up to the reputation of the school, or are students disengaged from school affairs?

As a new principal I found that a few key faculty tend to determine expectations for their colleagues and students. This "culture" then tends to define the way things are done around the school. The power of informal organization, however, does not diminish the principal's leadership responsibility to improve the school. It is wise to understand the current culture before proposing surgery and then to act with W. Somerset Maugham's advice in your ear: "It's a funny thing about life; if you refuse to accept anything but the best, you very often get it."

The culture of Cubberley High School was driven by an interesting mix of people and focused on the personal as well as the academic development of students. Its culmination was expressed by the presentation of "Senior Bowls" at graduation, engraved large silver bowls awarded by the faculty to six students who most personified the values of academic achievement *and* service to the school. Its mentors included the English chair and an English teacher, two counselors, the science chair, the math chair, a biology teacher, and the industrial technology chair.

Lying beneath the exalted horizons of most graduate courses are the job skills that enable new principals to succeed. Here are a few that worked for me:

1. Organize the school week by publishing for teachers every Friday afternoon the events of the next week, day by day. Include commendations and announcements. This document places everyone on the same page in a busy school.
2. Meet occasionally with the secretarial and custodial staff. They know some things about the school missed by teachers, and their work deserves recognition. One of the best heads at Cubberley was Tim Mellor, the chief custodian.
3. Close down the public address system when classes are in session.
4. Take your share of the dirty work; good example goes a long way.
5. Make the school look good; people will respond and gain pride. My first visible act as principal was to remove the vending machines in the entry foyer and replace them with art.
6. Develop new programs with teachers to improve instruction. Always have something going based on research to replace the status quo. Work with the departments most ready, and the others will come along. Incremental change tends to be more successful and lasting than dramatic, schoolwide initiatives that quickly lose steam.

At the end of my first year as principal, the day following graduation, I was exhausted but feeling affirmed. I had made my share of mistakes: misread a couple of teachers, pushed an unready department too hard to change, was too tough with some students and too easy with others, did not handle a parent conference well, and could have taken dozens of initiatives that time simply did not allow. But, on balance, the 180 days and 90 nights spent on school business had gone reasonably well for a novice principal.

The desk calendar, now a bit shopworn, falls open to Monday, June 21. The quotation at the bottom of the page reads, "We can finish nothing in this life: but we make a beginning, and bequeath a noble example." Not a bad thought for a new principal in June, even for one who was not quite a noble example.

Scott Thomson is with the National Policy Board for Educational Administration in Fairfax, Virginia.

Compromises

THEODORE R. SIZER

"Can you lend me a quarter?"

The stringy, smirking kid stood in front of his dormitory, addressing me as I climbed out of my car. It was May 1972. The headmaster-elect, I was making my once-a-week visit to Andover, still juggling the duties of a Harvard deanship with trying to figure out what this residential high school might be all about.

Cheeky? Yes. He had obviously been put up to this little request. His friends were visible at the dormitory windows, giggling. My predecessor was seen by many of the kids as aloof and formal, particularly during the last months as he was dying of cancer. No one would try to cadge a quarter off him.

So, what about this new guy, thirty-nine years old and only distantly a practicing school person? The kids must have sensed my awkwardness in the assemblies where I had first met them. They did not really know that I had not worked among adolescents since 1958, and then in an Australian grammar school, but they acutely sensed my rawness.

"Sure." I fumbled in my pocket and, mercifully, found a quarter. "Will I get it back?"

"Ummm." Laughter. "Of course. . . ." He took off. The dormitory windows dribbled guffaws. I felt like a turkey.

So much of my first year was like that. There was much to do of an administrative nature, both pushing ahead with good initiatives already resting on the faculty's agenda, merging the school (then for males only) with an adjacent school for young women, coping with putting together two wary faculties, calming a board of trustees still reeling from all the embarrassing newnesses foisted upon them by the 1960s. While none of this with adults was always easy, it was familiar stuff. I had coped with that and worse as a Harvard dean during the sixties. It was the cheeky kids that made me nervous.

One minute they were naughty Tom Sawyers hornswoggling a naive new headmaster, the next, hard headed student newspaper editors with carefully wrought opinions on demonstrably important matters. They did very dumb things, from constantly losing their books to taking LSD, and yet they pulled off smart things, not only in BC Calculus but also beyond, as when the seniors, largely drawn from the football team, quietly negotiated with their counterparts at the local high school a privately but firmly enforced smothering of rough teenaged rowdiness that had cropped up in the neighborhood.

They couldn't follow a simple and logical argument in history class one minute, and they saw deeply into a comparable matter the next. Many claimed that they knew that they were really in love and that sleeping with that freshman girl was an oh-so-adult expression of lifetime fidelity, and at the next moment they could deeply fathom the fear of a newcomer to the school from a foreign place (an American inner city or another country, for example) and subtly intuit what collective nurturing and befriending of that fresh arrival must be summoned.

Dumb and smart. Thoughtful and thoughtless. Narcissistic and empathic. All at once. Even in the same fifteen minutes.

By contrast, the graduate students in education that I had been teaching for over a decade were a dull lot, often too predictable. Adolescents? How do you school a person who is a boy one minute and a man the next, a girl at 9:00 A.M. and a woman at noon?

Collectively, the faculty members, veteran, skilled, and committed though they were, gave no help at all.

"We have to have rules at this school and we must consistently enforce them. The students have to learn that the world is a demanding place, that there are some things that are nonnegotiable. To waffle on standards is to hurt the youngsters. For us to fail as certain adults is to let this school drift into chaos. We must be clear. The rules must be clear. We know what these kids need. They want us to be firm. They learn from pushing against us. . . ."

"Our job is to get these kids to make good decisions on their own. They need practice at that. If we tell them what to do and when to study all the time, if we order their lives for them, we do them a disservice. We must stop incarcerating them in enforced dependency, we the rule-delivering jailers, they the cowed inmates. They'll revolt. Indeed, they already are in revolt, in this school at least, in a sneaky, remarkably polite sort of way. And they are not all alike and don't want to be treated alike. They deserve to take, they have to take more responsibility. . . ."

"There is a core of knowledge that every young person must know."

"Students should have some say in what they study. If they don't they will just go through the motions, mindlessly dishing back to us what we have dished out to them. They should be considered apprentices in learning, not vessels into which we pour our knowledge."

"How in God's name does a student who doesn't know anything know what he wants to study?"

"They're old enough to be left alone with their lives. For their own sakes we have got to get off their backs. Give them some respect, some privacy, for heaven's sake!"

"They are children. When they are at school, we must act in loco parentis. They can't be trusted, and every day they demonstrate that truth for all of us to see."

"Good grief, kids all over the world take responsibility. Read history. Adolescents have made a difference when they have been expected to make a difference in their lives. We are putting diapers on these young grown-ups."

"Where have you been? Do you know what some of the kids did over last weekend? Come off it. These youngsters aren't Joan of Arc. You just want to pretend they are to get yourself off the hot seat of telling them there are some standards around here."

So, the new headmaster wondered, how do you write the student handbook? Where do you draw the line? How do you cope with a student body drawn from many cultural quarters, where what is a crucial (if substantively trivial) symbol for one person (wearing a baseball cap all the time, for example) is an offense for another ("Don't wear your hat in the house"). How do you tell young people to be violent on the hockey rink ("Kill, Kill, Hate, Hate, Murder, Murder, Mutilate" from the cheerleaders) and to be nonviolent everywhere else? How do you talk of the sweetness of chastity and still gather around and support the girl who becomes pregnant?

Aren't there rules in this world? Or is everything spongily relative, the world rudderless? Can adults ever avoid the ubiquitous adolescent charge of hypocrisy? Can't we all depend on anything? If not, how, for Pete's sake, do you run a decent and happy and constructive school?

I was surprised during those first months at Andover to find the students more at ease with these ambiguities than were the faculty, but in time I learned better. They just faked at it more, probably because they did not know that their confusion wasn't just their own personal confusion. There is no more wisdom coming out of the mouths of adolescent babes than clarity on these matters emerging from a solemn faculty meeting. The hard fact, I soon learned, was that there would never be sharply etched answers, that, paradoxically, all of the questions being asked and answers given were, to some degree, correct.

In our culture, adolescence is, for better or worse, a deliberately gray area, a zone of inescapable ambiguity. The best teachers want their students both to develop habits of decent, informed, and thoughtful behavior and not to hurt themselves, indeed even be happy. The youngsters are groping, wanting at the same time autonomy and respect from their elders. Most of the world, however, is for them new, and their autonomous decisions are, not surprisingly, often dumb ones. The less respect the young people sense, the more grotesque is their pushing against their elders, from being merely cheeky to evolving into gangs that make sure that none are "dissed" without retribution.

As a result, high school is a seesaw, requiring here, giving choice there, being clear here, being deliberately reserved and ambiguous there. It is a place for kids trying out, being both girls and women, boys and men. It is tough for them and tough for their teachers (and their parents). It is never dull, and it is often scary, for young and old.

School is about making endless, wise compromises. There is no Rule, no Predictability. Adolescence denies that. But there is clarity sometimes, direction sometimes, freedom sometimes, empathy and caring and patience always. I learned that during my first year.

No, I never got that quarter back. In my confusion I had forgotten, of course, to ask the cadger his name.

THEODORE R. SIZER TEACHES AT BROWN UNIVERSITY IN RHODE ISLAND. HE IS THE DIRECTOR OF THE ANNENBERG INSTITUTE FOR SCHOOL REFORM AND CHAIRMAN OF THE COALITION OF ESSENTIAL SCHOOLS.

The Monk in the Schoolhouse

BRUCE A. SEGALL

My wife, Dorothea, and I were born and raised in the New York metropolitan area. When I received the appointment as principal of Alfred-Almond Junior-Senior High School, it was with great joy but a bit of anxiety. Almond is a small rural town in upstate New York, beautiful but culturally very different from what Dorothea and I were accustomed to. Alfred, on the other hand, is a university town with cultural and athletic opportunities that made our adjustment to the area much easier.

I vividly remember that first day, sitting by the tennis courts in front of the school and having this feeling of calm and peace come over me. It was as if someone had taken me and let some of the air out of my balloon. I could feel the slower pace of life. This same experience occurred again later that day when I got ready to leave for my temporary home. It was 5:00 P.M. I remember getting that awful feeling urbanites get at "rush hour." I would surely get caught right in the middle of it. I dashed out of school and drove quickly down the road. As I moved up the ramp to Route 17, I looked around and, to my amazement, there was not a car in sight. Needless to say, it was a very pleasant ride home that evening and every evening thereafter.

THE TEACHERS

What made my first year so memorable were the teachers. They were an extraordinary group of dedicated professionals who took an idealistic young principal under their wings. The friendships and relationships built up over the years are still very much a part of my life. I remember Jan, a dedicated English teacher who would never be out of class because her lessons were so individualized that it took two to three pages of instructions for each class. She spent hours correcting papers and preparing lessons. She and her husband became lifelong friends to Dorothea and me. She helped me see each student as an individual with unique needs.

Mike was a very special person. The room lit up when he walked in. Caring and charismatic, he reminded me that as I was leading the troops through the wilderness, he was killing the snakes and alligators. He was a social studies teacher who helped me start an alternative program for high-risk kids. Many years later he would die of cancer. I still miss him.

Bob was my jock-friend. We loved to play basketball together and talk about administration. He became the assistant principal in a neighboring school. One day Bob and Mike handed in a discipline referral on a fictitious student named, "Barney Rubble" and signed Jan's name. Every day for a week I called "Barney" over the P.A. system. Finally, on the fifth day I got on the P.A. and said that if Barney Rubble did not report to the office he would be in serious trouble. A few minutes later Mike and Bob came laughing into my office. I had been accepted into the culture of the school. Everything would work out.

One of the most moving expressions of the relationships that were being built up with the teachers was the presence of so many of them and their spouses when I bought a house and moved into the district. More than half the staff helped me move twice, once to a temporary home and finally to my permanent residence. I will always remember their kindness in providing the labor and food at this important time in my life.

COSLOS

Coslos was a family restaurant down the road from the school. Every so often we would have a T.G.I.F. get-together after school. I believed strongly in building a foundation of trust among the teachers. I also strongly believed in building community. Social affairs can be very important in that total process and enhance the quality of the work we do. Shortly before he died, Mike told me that Coslos had more to do with my success than anything else. Some of my staff didn't agree with everything I was doing, but at least they could sit down with me in an informal setting and share their thoughts and aspirations. Coslos went a long way in helping to build a community of educators with a common mission.

A SOCCER GAME/THE SITDOWN

Two of the biggest challenges I had to face as a new principal were in the area of discipline. The first dealt with a soccer game early in the fall. Our team had a number of incidents of unsportsmanlike conduct. At one point there were some actual fights. I had become increasingly alarmed at the behavior of the student-athletes, and the fighting was the last straw. After speaking privately with the coach and athletic director, I called an assembly of the entire school and announced my decision. I was suspending the entire team from competition for one game and would not permit them to play again until they proved to me and the coach that they were ready to play the game properly. Shortly after the assembly, the captains and the coach came to me to say they had learned their lesson and were ready to play the game in a sportsmanlike manner.

The second challenge came unexpectedly. Alfred-Almond did not have a written student handbook. I had always been a strong proponent of such a document because it clearly lays out the rules and the consequences. I spent time with the staff drafting the rules and had them typed up and printed in manual form. I called an assembly for the student body and explained the need for a handbook and rules. As the students left the assembly, I noticed that many were walking rather slowly. I left the room for a few minutes and when I returned, there were about one hundred students still there engaged in a "sitdown." They said they objected to the handbook and were not going to classes. I had to think fast, so I told them they had five minutes to get to class or they would be suspended, but I also said that I would be happy to meet with any individual or his/her representative during lunch, study period, or after school. Gradually, all the students returned to their classes. Several students did show up, and we discussed their concerns. Each year thereafter the student council reviewed the handbook before it was printed.

THE DREAMS

I am an idealist. I always have been and I hopefully always will be. I dream about the perfect school, and that first year I had several dreams.

The first had to do with the notion of authority. From my theological studies I was aware of the concept of the "Primus Inter Pares" or the "First Among Equals." Although this was only my first year in public administration, I felt that the idea of a lone chief on top of bureaucratic order was dissatisfying and unproductive. I wanted my staff to know that, like them, I too was an educator. I wanted to help them in any way I could to become better educators. I substituted frequently, lectured occasionally, and wanted to teach periodically, which I did a few years later. I tried to use memos, announcements, and assemblies as learning experiences. Although a teacher, I had responsibilities beyond the individual classroom and therefore, I had to be the "first" among teachers. As the principal educator I wanted to provide the instructional, ethical, and dynamic leadership that was necessary to make our school absolutely first rate.

My second dream had to do with building a real community of educators. I needed to lay a foundation of trust so that real change could take place. I needed to *model* this trust and establish relationships in such a way that we could say with sincerity and integrity that "we are a community of educators bound together by a common purpose."

My third dream was to work toward a comprehensive evaluation program that would involve a multiplicity of perceptions on observable teacher behavior. Evaluation programs are usually limited because they involve only the perceptions of the supervisor, however competent he/she may be. I wanted to enlarge on this by including self, peer, and student evaluations along with the supervisory ones. With this kind of information matrix, we could begin to focus on our strengths and improve on our weaknesses.

THE MONASTERY

Before I began my career in education, I was a Marianist Brother for six years. The Marianists were a teaching order of Brothers and Sisters. During those years I developed a prayer life that became essential to me as a person and especially as I began my career as a high school principal. Less than an hour from my school was Mount Savior Monastery that I had come to know before my appointment. After my appointment it became my oasis. Several times a year I had the need to journey there—discovering in silence and solitude ways to cope with the pressures, trials, and tribulations of my profession. Long, silent walks and journal writings about my life and profession became critical life supports for me that first year and are still, seventeen years later. When I moved back downstate after eight years, I looked first for another monastery within an hour's drive. Behind my desk on the wall in my office is a picture which I asked my sister-in-law to draw for me. The picture shows a man walking down from the mountain into a classroom full of children. The title of the picture is, "The Monk in the Schoolhouse."

MY FAMILY

In addition to my prayer life, my family has always been instrumental in my ability to cope with the stress of my job. One cannot overestimate the value of a happy home life. Having a loving wife and wonderful children to come home to every evening puts a job and a profession into proper focus. Learning how to be a good husband to Dorothea and a father to Ken, Christiane, and later to Brad has been tremendously fulfilling. While I certainly recognize and accept the variety of roles a woman can play in modern life, I can honestly say that having Dorothea as wife, friend, and fellow parent was absolutely essential to my initial success as a principal.

Equally essential were those moments each evening and on weekends as I watched and played with my children. As I flip through years of memories, I can still see them playing with the pots and pans in the kitchen that first year at Alfred-Almond.

BRUCE SEGALL IS THE PRINCIPAL AT MAHWAH HIGH SCHOOL IN MAHWAH, NEW JERSEY.

The Time I Spend

PATRICIA McRAE

I did not move up through the system in the lighthouse district in which I now work. I came from Alaska where I had been a teacher and then principal/teacher in small (some might say minuscule) rural Alaskan towns for nine years. I moved from teaching and principaling in a school of thirty-five students K–12, to Jackson Park Elementary, a school of 450 students on the Olympic Peninsula in Washington. The staff at my new school surpasses the number of students and parents combined at my previous school. There was a larger population of caribou in Cantwell, Alaska, than humans; and worries about children's safety as they got off the school bus focused on grizzly bears in the area as opposed to child snatchers or drive-by shootings. But whether in a big school or small, in the bush of Alaska or on the outskirts of a metropolis, the principal functions as the person who ensures the children's safety and security, the person who keeps the goals, beliefs, and vision of the school community dynamic, and the person who sets the tone for leadership and learning. The biggest differences I have faced have been more in the amount of time spent on individual tasks than in their content.

Of all I have dealt with this year, time has been the challenge with which I have struggled the most. When payday comes I find that I think more about the time it will take me to go to the bank and deposit the money than I think about the sum of money itself. Because I have always loved my work and have felt my schools were a second home, I spend much time at them.

Up north my children and my husband and I all worked and learned at the same school. Now that we are mainstream Americans, we all go our separate ways every morning in two different cars and two different school buses to get to four different schools. We arrive at home in four different vehicles at four different times every afternoon. I am invariably the last one to arrive.

Evening meetings are frequent for me, and I leave our home after eating only to return after my family has gone to sleep. In Alaska I worked sixty to seventy hours a week, but the majority of weekend hours were spent on classroom projects or all-school field trips to "town." (Town was Fairbanks or Anchorage, two hundred miles either way.) These days the majority of my after school hours aren't spent on field trips or bulletin boards. They are spent on survival. As a full-time principal in a school of 450, there are no all-school field trips, a reality I find very frustrating since "town" is here. I want to take ALL 450 kids to a play at the theatre, but to do so would cost more than our school budget for supplies. My office usually looks as though a tornado has hit the area and meeting deadlines for the numerous tasks that go along with this job has been one of my challenges. In Alaska my school employed four other full-time staff members besides myself, and I was married to one of them. I knew when a fellow staff member had a hangnail or a poor night's sleep. When I began at Jackson Park last August, I was positive that I would be able to talk with every staff member every day and that I would visit every classroom every day. I have found that such a goal is not practical. Ensuring time for communication while doing an adequate job of management is the balance I am still trying to achieve. Having an "open door" when a parent, staff member, or student needs me will always take first place, but that doesn't replace the accountability for paperwork, meetings, and deadlines.

Late hours, a messy office, and the lack of all-school field trips aside, I love this confounding job. I love it when I am at the mall or the grocery store and one of my Jackson Park Patriots sees me and whispers in an excited voice, "Mom! It's the PRINCIPAL!" These occasions remind me of the enormous responsibility I have in living up to my students' expectations. I was immensely gratified the other day as I walked through a sixth grade classroom and one of the students (whose mother I have had to call about less than pleasant matters many times) said, "Ms. McRae, my mother likes to talk to you on the phone!" The feeling is mutual. Everything about us, our lives, and our experiences are different, yet we have found that we have a lot in common. This relationship is what enables us to work together for her child's success.

In my first year as an elementary principal, I have attempted to be a person who can share the thoughts I have about the strengths of this school community, and I have tried to model my belief in the power of listening, caring, and learning. My staff has supported me, and I feel great about that. I truly believe that the children who attend Jackson Park School couldn't ask for a better place to grow and become what they hope to be. And neither could I, but the clock is still running.

PATRICIA MCRAE IS PRINCIPAL AT JACKSON PARK ELEMENTARY SCHOOL IN BREMERTON, WASHINGTON.

The First Hundred Days

JOSEPH C. SEGAR

It was 1963, for me the first of twenty-six years at Shady Hill. As a rookie school head I had a lot to learn and, although none of us was aware of it, the country was on the verge of a series of catastrophic events. Approaching the little grey cottages of Shady Hill's campus early that July morning I wasn't at all sure the search committee had found the right man. Would I have something special to offer this unique and distinguished school? How would I measure up in Cambridge, the "Athens of the Western World"?

I felt that my first task was to begin to understand the people who made the school function. In July there was little activity . . . a small summer school for academic enrichment supplied the only students and faculty. The skeleton office staff and the groundspeople were busy with all those jobs schools have to complete before Labor Day. I sent a general invitation for teachers and staff to come see me, and many did. My opening ploy in those conversations was, "What do you think I need to know about you and where you fit in at Shady Hill?" And my final question, as the discussion concluded was, " What advice do you have for me?" Those talks with staff were immensely useful to me, and I believe they laid strong foundations for our work on behalf of children. I discovered the generosity of Shady Hill people and their pride in the school; each talk helped me enormously, and soon I was developing some insights about what should happen next. By mid-August I had begun to know the faculty and staff, some of the overseers, and a few students and parents.

Two unscheduled visits I recall with special pleasure. The first came from grinning Eddie Pratt, then headmaster of the neighboring Browne and Nichols School, who strolled across his playing fields to introduce himself and offer his help.

The second was from a very tall man with craggy features who had to duck his head as he entered my office one afternoon. He seemed familiar, and I thought I should know him, but he didn't give his name. He knew who I was, and it soon became clear that he was a school parent because he talked about his sons and his hopes for them. Our conversation rambled; he was cordial, tremendously well-informed and somewhat opinionated. I enjoyed the visit and as he rose to leave I realized . . . belatedly . . . that he was John Kenneth Galbraith.

The parents were an impressive lot and, for a first-year school head, sometimes intimidating. I learned quickly that these people did not come to Shady Hill wearing their laurels or their titles: they came as mothers and fathers, with all the hopes, all the fears that any parent brings to her or his child's school. What they wanted was the best possible experience for their son or daughter. And since they had a close, working relationship with schools and schooling, they were apt to be more understanding, more tolerant than many. It was sometimes difficult to convince teachers that they were the experts when they sat down with a parent in the classroom after school to have a conference about a student's progress. No matter how distinguished, the parents came to school to learn from the teacher.

Opening faculty meetings, the first day of school, the first overseers' meeting, the first all-school assembly, the new parents dinner, even the first fire drill . . . it was all unfamiliar territory for me, and I moved through those early weeks in something of a fog, trying hard to be a leader, not forgetting that I was very much a learner. I tried to honor the resolutions I'd made during the summer. "Think before you decide." "Be a listener." "Remember everyone's name." "Know the faculty by Halloween and the students by Thanksgiving." "Keep a diary." "Don't get bogged down in fragments; look for the big picture." "Visit classes regularly." "Write appreciative notes; be lavish with praise and stingy with criticism."

But things happened. A teacher wanted to introduce a major new element into the curriculum. Immediately. (Not yet. I need to know whether quality is being sacrificed.) A parent wanted her daughter excused from sports to ride because she was destined to be an Olympic equestrienne. (No. Part of the value of sports for children at this age is participating in a joint endeavor.) The student council wanted to install a soft drink vending machine. (No. Distracting, unhealthy, trash-producing.) I wanted to keep my door open, to be available, but I was frequently being interrupted. I was inefficient and I seldom got out of the office to visit classes or go to games. My vision of myself as the benevolent headmaster was fading.

And then, on November 22, in Dallas, optimism was caught in the cross hairs of an assassin's rifle. That Friday and throughout the weekend that followed, the dreadful events were played and replayed on the television screens of every home in America. Shady Hill students—the eldest was only fourteen—were frightened. They had seen the effect of these events on the adults in their lives, and they needed to know that someone would take care of them, that their world would not disintegrate.

The first thing on Monday morning, I called most of the students and their teachers to the Hall. We talked, we sat silent, we listened to each other's reactions, we cried. I stood in the midst of that crowd, trying to be the understanding, reassuring figure everyone wanted. Could I explain the unexplainable? Could I make sense from senseless violence? Certainly not. But something needed to be said, and I tried. Afterward, a teacher slipped onto the piano bench and began softly to play, and we all sang, softly at first and then with the increasing strength we gathered from each other . . . "Mine eyes have seen the glory of the coming of the Lord . . . " Then, as if it had been rehearsed, each class silently followed its teacher out of the Hall.

It was then, in those forty minutes, that I felt I was going to become the leader of the school. Not when I proposed a new system of marking to the faculty. Not when I suggested to the overseers that we build a new field house. Not when I hosted the new parents dinner for the first time. But that day, just before Thanksgiving, in the third month of my first year, with the same lump in my throat, the same questions in my mind, the same ache in my heart that everyone had, I learned what it meant to be a school head.

JOSEPH SEGAR LIVES AND WORKS IN BARNSTABLE, MASSACHUSETTS.

Hopeful to Hectic

MARK WARREN SEGAR

*E*veryone knew who I was, of course. The teachers, students, parents, and custodial and office staffs all greeted me by name that first day. I remember a sense of imbalance welling up, a kind of professional vertigo as I looked at all those welcoming, wondering faces with names not yet securely attached.

I was sure that most of them wanted me to succeed; certain, too, that some of them had special interests to guard, maybe even axes to grind, and that they would be anxious to know where I stood on a whole host of issues facing the school and its community. All those projected hopes, unvoiced but no less real, piled high on the in-basket of expectations and emotions that met me as I began this new and different work.

I had come to The Common School from state government, from the governor's staff where I'd worked on state policy for education and youth services. I'd been eager to get away from state politics for some time. I wanted to work with real families again, with individual children instead of statistical populations and groups. Politicians constantly wondering about the extent of their minimal obligations to children had strained my commitment to child advocacy and early education. The opportunity to lead a small, experimental school was timely, a chance to move away from questions like "What can we afford?" toward "What's the best we might do?"

And besides, the governor I devotedly worked for had lost his reelection bid and then died suddenly while still in office. His successor seemed an unlikely patron for the liberal likes of me.

My political past followed me from the State House to the schoolhouse. Who was I to head this school, to lead this faculty? What values would a veteran of the political trenches bring—and project—in the hitherto untainted role of school leader? I hadn't been a teacher in years, and I'd never taught long division.

So I'd planned carefully for that first opening day. I would be outside to greet all the arriving students and parents. I would spend the bulk of the morning in classrooms. I would be out with my sneakers on for recess. I would be visible, engaged, observing, welcoming, offering a hand.

Things went from hopeful to hectic in a hurry. First my wife called to say that her car was dead in our driveway. She was late for work. Our boys (already bearing the ignominious weight of having Dad for a principal) were late for their first day, and I would have to drive home and pick up everyone. School opened without me, essentially. (No doubt some thought I was isolated in my office already.)

By the time I got back there were other problems. A toilet had backed up. No custodian was available. Did I know where the plunger was? On it went through the day to faculty meeting, where my bumbling efforts to ingratiate myself with humor met with puzzled (not even bemused) silence. It was a rocky start.

I thought the first few months should be a time for observation, for gathering ideas, for listening to opinions, for constructing a set of ideas about challenges and priorities for the future. Others immediately thought otherwise. When would I move from being a facilitator to being a leader? How soon could my ideas for curriculum be implemented? Any luck yet on new sources of funding?

I kept responding and reacting, eager to solve, to soothe, to please. It took me a while to figure out that I wouldn't be able to work this way for long. Or that if I did, I'd never accomplish anything significant or coherent. I needed help.

Sometimes I think that people who become principals aren't very good at asking for help. We tend to be the types who, when confronted with a problem, respond with "I'll tackle it," or "I'll get right on it," or—if we've made a little progress—"You're right about that. Let's work on it together." We want to get things done. We have faith in our own ideas and abilities. We like to get right to work. A worthy attitude, but not necessarily always what's needed. And untenable when the demands pile up, as they did so quickly for me.

So I called my father and another principal and spilled all sorts of concerns and questions into the phone, hoping for good answers from these wise and experienced leaders. The similarity of their responses was startling. Neither of them had answers to offer. Instead they had questions. Question after question in response to mine, probing for details about the culture of my school, about the nature of the particular challenges I faced, about my own tentative ideas and strategies for next steps.

Suddenly in the midst of those phone calls, the connections began to form clearly in my mind—between a belief in questions as the essential units of learning and a commitment to leadership as something other than coming up with all the solutions by myself. Reflecting on all the questions my interrogators had for me, I thought back to how much of my own schooling and training had emphasized answers, had stressed getting it right alone. I thought about my own school's philosophical commitment to discovery learning and collaborative problem solving for students. I even dredged up from college studies the memory of Lao Tze's wisdom (already invoked, of course, by Roland Barth and many other experienced principals, as I would come to learn) that of a great leader the people will all say, "We did this ourselves."

Awash in realization and reverie, I finished the calls as politely as I could, already feeling the press of unmanageable expectations beginning to lift. A way of working successfully and sustainably at this still wonderful job was beginning to take shape. It has served me well, and I remain grateful to those model question askers from my first year.

MARK WARREN SEGAR IS HEAD OF WAYNFLETE SCHOOL IN PORTLAND, MAINE.